DRIFTED ASTRAY

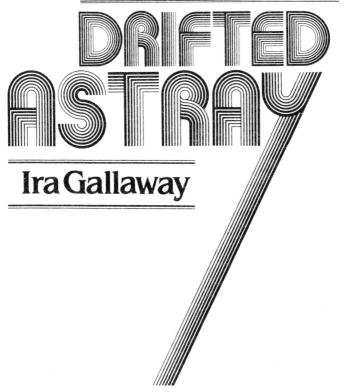

Returning the Church to Witness & Ministry

DRIFTED ASTRAY

Ira Gallaway

Abingdon Press

Nashville

Drifted Astray: Returning the Church to Witness and Ministry

Library of Congress Cataloging in Publication Data

Gallaway, Ira, 1923-
  Drifted astray.
  Includes bibliographical references.
  1. Church renewal—Methodist Church. 2. Mission of the
church. 3. Holy Spirit. 4. Methodist Church—Doctrinal and
controversial works. I. Title.
BX8331.2.G34   1983   262'.7   82-20595

ISBN 0-687-11186-2

MANUFACTURED BY THE PARTHENON PRESS AT
NASHVILLE, TENNESSEE, UNITED STATES OF AMERICA

*Dedicated
to my wife and co-worker
SALLY
This book is a product of
our ministry together*

Contents

Foreword

D*rifted Astray* is a book whose time has come and is, in fact, long overdue. Dr. Gallaway speaks out in straightforward and honest reality, saying what many leaders of the church have been saying privately, but which few are willing to risk expounding publicly.

The author is recognized as one of the nation's most outstanding pastors, but he speaks out of the perspective of a former judge and layman who came to know Christ through the ministry of the church. He speaks boldly for a new vision of the church which liberates it for ministry and redemption in the lives of people. He speaks as a prophet and modern-day reformer.

As a layman in The United Methodist Church, I identify with and support Dr. Gallaway's thesis. If our denomination is to meet the needs of its people, it must wake up, listen, and follow the prescriptions that Dr. Gallaway sets forth.

Fourteen years ago, ten million Methodists and a million Evangelical United Brethren merged to form The United Methodist Church. Since then, during a time of national population expansion, the net loss in membership has been nearly double the entire E.U.B. denomination. Could it be that a church all caught up in structure and process and more concerned with social issues than with the whole gospel just isn't relevant to the needs of its people? Will people respond to a ministry more grounded in secular values than in biblical perspective? Has the concept of "pluralism" been redefined to give legitimacy to a system of "theological elitism"?

Dr. Gallaway speaks directly and with conviction to the church's response to many social issues of our day—issues where church leadership and biblical foundations are not in mutual harmony. A church whose leadership is more attuned to the secular solutions to social problems is not a church free to minister in accordance with Christ's teachings.

Many criticize in order to tear down, but Dr. Gallaway offers a constructive alternative by challenging the church to examine itself from within and to analyze its ministry after reflection on the Bible and through a freedom which allows the Holy Spirit to speak to pastors and laity alike. He believes, as do I, that The United Methodist Church remains as one of the greatest institutions for spiritual revival in America. Its stated theology, mixed with true social concern, provides a firm foundation to meet the spiritual and physical needs of a hungry world. Its ecumenical orientation gives it the flexibility and adaptability to minister to a diverse and pluralistic world.

The laity of the church hungers for the style of national leadership and openness for ministry as described in this book. *Drifted Astray* should be read by both pastor and laity. Its message can help bring reformation to the church and undergird both clergy and laity in ministering Christ's redemption to the world.

John Grant
Tampa, Florida
September 12, 1982

John Grant is a lawyer and member of the Florida House of Representatives. He is a leading layman in The United Methodist Church, having been a delegate to World, General, Jurisdictional, and Annual Conferences. He served as president of the Florida Conference of United Methodist Men and for ten years directed the Leesburg Retreats, one of the largest laymen's retreats in the denomination.

He is currently a member of the Board of Managers of the American Bible Society, and he has served on the general boards of Missions, Laity, and Discipleship of The United Methodist Church.

Introduction

Twenty-five years ago, I was a young businessman making my way in the world of secular success, while at the same time maintaining a rather tenuous connection with religion—not faith—as a nominal Christian in The Methodist Church. Oh, I served on the board of my church, had served as a charge lay leader in the past on the conference board of the laity, and was then serving along with Sally, my wife, as co-president of a large young adult Sunday school class. But, though I had some of the outward trappings of the Christian religion—church attendance and apparent acceptance of the moral norms of the Christian faith—I was a nominal Christian. I adapted to the requirements of getting ahead in life, worked hard, did my job, and was discreet about my indiscretions. But I now know that in all of this, God was working in my life.

I was in management in a growing independent oil

company, moving ahead with the company, and was paying for a four-bedroom-three-bath home in suburban Dallas. In all outward appearances I was not only moving toward achievement and success, but was already successful. Yet, deep within my heart and mind was a restlessness, a sense of emptiness which business deals, clubs, social diversions, or whatever, did not seem to quiet or fill for long. Had you asked me to speak rationally and openly about that which was missing in my life, I would have probably told you that nothing was missing.

It was during this time that I first began to truly hear the radicalness of the gospel of Jesus Christ. Dean Eugene B. Hawk, then in his seventies, former pastor, teacher, seminary dean and university administrator, was the teacher of our adult church school class. Among many bits of wisdom and truth that he shared, were these:

"Jesus Christ is the key to understanding history."

"Jesus Christ is the fulcrum of history."

"You will never know who you are until you know Jesus Christ."

"Paul is one of the great minds of civilization."

I am sure that other preachers and/or teachers may have said some or all of those same things in my hearing before, but I had not heard them. The Holy Spirit began to take these thoughts and use them as leaven in the confusion and uncertainty of my life—and of our lives as a family. Had you interrogated me about the Christian faith at this time, my answers would have been at best, evasive.

"Are you a Christian, Ira?"

"Sure, I joined The Methodist Church when I was thirteen."

"Do you believe in Jesus Christ?"

"Certainly, I believe that Jesus Christ lived about two thousand years ago and the story in the Bible about him is essentially true."

"Do you know Jesus Christ personally, Ira?"

"Are you kidding? Jesus has been dead for over nineteen hundred years! How can you possibly know someone personally who is dead?"

"How then, does being a Christian affect your life?"

"Well, I guess it makes me a better person; but, I am not sure that I could be specific about any particular effect on my life."

Then, for the first time in my life I began to read the New Testament with a seeking heart and mind. Occasionally I talked with others, including my wife, about God, faith, and Jesus Christ. I had read the Bible as a boy in Sunday school, but at the age of seventeen, when I graduated from high school, I dropped out of church altogether. I did not again relate to the church in any regular fashion until I was twenty-seven and was serving as a judge in my home county. Then my reinvolvement with the church was pragmatic. If I were to be a successful politician in West Texas, at that time at least, it would be essential that I have solid religious connections. I would probably have dropped out of church again, when I left politics for the business world, but my wife who was raised outside the church, had found something that was meaningful in her life and she was not willing to give it up. It was in this milieu that I began to read the New Testament and think about Jesus Christ as the key to history, as well as the key to understanding and fulfillment in my own life. I was thirty-two years old at the time, married, and the father of four children.

Over a period of months there developed an "oughtness"—an imperative in my life, within my heart and mind—that I must do something additional about my faith. At the same time, it still did not make sense to me that I could really know Jesus Christ. But, life as it was, though good and desirable in outward circumstances, was not satisfying and truly good.

Along with this imperative, came the recurring thought that not only should I do something about my relationship with God, but should I give my life to Him, whatever that meant, it would mean serving Him in some vocational way. A side of me was repelled at that idea, because I did not especially like religious people or the moral legalisms that I understood them to represent. Further, preachers as a whole, with very limited exceptions, were just not my cup of tea.

And yet, the imperative, the idea, the thought, would not leave me. All kinds of events and happenings, unrelated to faith or religion in a formal sense, began to cause me to return to thoughts of Jesus Christ and His meaning for my life. Finally, I came to sense that if I did not make some specific decision about Jesus Christ and God in my life, I would actually lose my life.

So it was, that the time of my conscious commitment to Jesus Christ as revealer of God also included a commitment to follow Him—to serve Him—and to begin at least the process of entering the ministry of the church. Frankly, this was not a clear and unambiguous commitment, without doubts and fears. I well recall the events during a Holy Week service, with Bishop William C. Martin preaching, when my wife and I moved to the altar to surrender our lives to Jesus Christ and to begin our journey into ministry. My thoughts went something like this: "God you had better meet me at that altar, or I am an utter fool. There is so much that I don't know—am not sure about—so much that needs to be changed in my life that I will fall flat on my face unless you are real somehow. God, you had better be there—to accept me—to change me—to lead me."

I do not remember all the details of that evening, but this one thing I do remember, when I and my wife knelt at the altar of God's church in trusting and doubting faith, and reached out to Him, we began to understand in our hearts and inner beings that He had always been reaching out to us. *He was there!* I do not want to argue, prove, or conjecture about how—but He was there! We had become Christians under construction—saying YES to what God had long beforehand begun in our lives. We had followed the teaching of Sam Shoemaker, without ever having heard of Sam Shoemaker. We had "surrendered as much of ourselves as we understood, to as much of Christ as we understood"[1] and by an act of the will had begun our covenant journey with the Creator and Redeemer of the universe—the God and Father of our Lord Jesus Christ. By the way, we have found this teaching of Dr. Shoemaker—"to surrender as much of yourself as you understand to as much of Christ as you understand"—to be a good pattern or model to follow daily as we seek to grow and mature as disciples of Jesus Christ.

The day we moved to the altar we did not become completed Christians with a settled theology that gave us all the answers to the ethical and moral dilemmas of our lives or of our time, but we did begin a journey with the living God. We began to sense and know what it was to experience the living reality of the living Christ. We tasted the reality of life, the truth of life in Christ, having known death without Him, and this life-or-death alternative grabbed hold of us and began to make sense.

Within months we sold our home, and I was licensed to preach and entered seminary—the world of Barth and Brunner, Bultmann and Tillich, Niebuhr and Rauschenbusch. The Gospel stories which had led me to Christ became subject to the scalpel of the higher critic and the form critic. I heard of the God without myth, of the God who is the ground of our being, and the leap of faith which is necessary to find Him. While I understood part of all this, at the same time I sensed that somehow the attitude or direction of much of the theology with which I was confronted did not ring true. It did not seem historically true to the New Testament's witness that God had revealed Himself in Jesus Christ and that through the birth, life, death, and resurrection of Jesus Christ He had made new life possible for me. Was Jesus God's gift to me, and to all who came to Him seeking faith? Yes! I sensed, I knew, that the story of Jesus Christ was not basically mythical in character, but historical and true as recorded in Scripture. I did not come to this conviction out of any doctrine of the inerrancy of Scripture, a doctrine that I had never even heard of before entering seminary. My conviction came from the witness of God's Spirit with my spirit that I had been touched by the truth and light of God and His life. (See Rom. 8:15-16.)

Seminary days were difficult for me. A great deal of that difficulty was my fault, because I often reacted instead of responded to the teaching and to some of the teachers. In my growing conviction that I had experienced God Himself through faith in Jesus Christ, I often failed to live and witness in the Spirit of the Christ I had come to know. All in all, however, I am grateful for my seminary experience; it equipped me to begin to study theology, and to develop an understanding of the Christian faith and its meaning for me and the world in which I live. In other ways, seminary training tended to make Jesus Christ and the Christian faith subject to a rationalistic and man-centered understanding of life. There were exceptions, both in teachers and in teaching, but the mood and the mind-set of the day was to subject the Word of God to the mind of man, and not to submit the mind of man to the Word of God. Today, after twenty-five years in the ministry—as student, pastor, administrator, district superintendent, general board executive, and seeking disciple of Jesus Christ—I have come more and more to see the wisdom and rightness of submitting myself to the Word of God and to the leadership of His Spirit in my life. This does not mean that I must turn my back on historical criticism or cease to use God-given reason, but it is to say, as taught by Scripture, that Scripture is preeminently the basic resource and foundation of teaching about the Christian faith. "All Scripture is inspired by God and profitable for teaching, for reproof, for correction, for training in righteousness; that the man of God may be adequate, equipped for every good work" (II Tim. 3:16-17). It is also to concur with the teaching of John Wesley, founder of Methodism and the key leader in the renewal of Christian life and faith in eighteenth-century England. "I allow no other rule, whether of faith or of practice, than the Holy Scriptures."[2]

In this introduction, I have attempted to sketch a witness of how God worked in my life to lead me to His salvation and into His ministry. The guiding force in my life is a desire to have all men and women come to know Jesus Christ as revealer of God and as personal Savior and Lord of life. It is my deep conviction that He is the key to life and the fulcrum of history.

It is also my considered, though reluctant, conviction that there is much in the institution, structure, and teaching of the denomination of which I am a part which hinders both the propagation of the Good News of Jesus Christ and its acceptance by many people in the world today. I see an imperative need for the liberation of the church for witness and ministry, so that many more may become disciples and witnesses for Jesus Christ. As there was once an "oughtness" in my life, which I came to realize was the Holy Spirit leading me to God, so there is now an "oughtness" which impels me to attempt a prophetic word to and about the church and its witness and ministry in our day. It has been a growing conviction over a number of years, and if I am to be true to the Lord whom I serve, then speak I must.

Because I know there will be disagreement with much of what I say—particularly on the part of some who are in leadership roles in our church, especially and including some of the bishops and the staffs of the general boards, it is with some trepidation and anxiety that I attempt to write as a prophet. But I am also a loyal and faithful son of the church—the church in which I found faith and have been given the high privilege and opportunity of service and ministry. I propose to speak the truth as God reveals it to me and as I understand that truth, in the hope that what I say may in some measure liberate the church for witness and ministry to a greater degree and more effective way for our time. I invite you to reflect on and respond to what I have written in the hope that it will speak creatively to the mission and ministry of the church in today's world.

PART ONE

*The
Nature of the
Church*

I

To Know Jesus Christ

But the thing a man does practically believe (and this often enough without asserting it even to himself, much less to others); the thing a man does practically lay to heart, and know for certain, concerning his vital relations to the mysterious Universe, and his duty and destiny there, that is in all cases the primary thing for him, and creatively determines all the rest.
                                                            —*Thomas Carlyle*

If we are to liberate the Christian church for witness and ministry, we must again decide what we believe about Jesus Christ. With all the talk, in our denomination at least, about pluralism in theology and doctrine, a pervasive idea or mind-set keeps surfacing which seems to preclude any definitive position about the divinity and humanity, the person and work of Jesus Christ. While I certainly recognize that no simplistic way can explain the Incarnation to the mind of modern man, I am convinced that until the church again preaches and teaches the orthodox or evangelical view of the historical Jesus Christ as God's mighty act in history to redeem a fallen humanity, there will be no renewal of faith and no infusion of redeeming power through the church. Further, it is not enough to teach about Jesus Christ; we must come to know in our hearts and minds the One in whom we believe, else there will be no renewal or liberation. He is the *Liberator*.

We live in an age which has become increasingly secular, relativistic in its moral and ethical understanding, and prejudiced, even to intolerance, toward any dogma or orthodoxy in matters of faith and morals. In such an age, it may be difficult indeed to persuade the leadership of the church to become infectious partisans for Jesus Christ as the God who has come among us.

When I was first enrolled in seminary, I discovered that any positive attempt to witness to faith in terms of being "born again" into the family of God through repentance and acceptance of Jesus Christ as Savior and Lord was likely to be branded as simplistic and fundamentalistic in attitude and theology. In fact, it was the accepted attitude of a number of teachers in the seminary to challenge everything an incoming student affirmed in faith, until that student was pressured to rebuild his or her own faith in "a more rational and theologically acceptable" model. While I accept the disciplines of theological study, reflection, reasoning, probing, and questioning one's faith, I am convinced that the rationalistic and superior attitude taken by many who teach a more dialectic and secular—sometimes even humanistic theology—is not helpful to the struggling and immature student who is trying to develop a sound faith and theology.

I will always remember and be grateful for a statement of Bishop William C. Martin at the opening chapel of my seminary experience. The bishop said, and I can still remember the comfort of his words as they later came to mean much to me: "Do not throw away or discard any aspect of your own faith, no matter how it may be challenged or questioned by your teachers here; that is, until you are sure that what is being projected in its place is better or more true than what you already hold!" Also, I am most grateful for several seminary professors who were patient with my immature and sometimes overzealous witness to my own faith experience and beginning theological perceptions. I have come to see, in retrospect, that God used a number of my professors in seminary to stretch my mind and enlarge my understanding of the Christian faith as well as my vision of what it means to live as a disciple of Jesus Christ.

I have also come to the conclusion in the light of my experience in seminary and as a churchman in various roles of leadership for the last twenty-five years, that there is a new kind of fundamentalism which is threatening to the historical faith and to the renewal of the church in these last years of the twentieth century. It seems to me that fundamentalism has always been more of an attitude or spirit of judgment than it has been a set code of doctrine or morality. Certainly, not many classical fundamentalists are within mainline Protestantism today. But I perceive that there is a fundamentalistic attitude often held by the modern secular-humanist, the modern liberal determinist, which rules out any acceptance of the transcendent God revealing Himself in Incarnation, or of a God who deals with His creation through redemption and reconciliation in history. This new fundamentalism looks much more toward the exercise of power in the church, through the use of political and secular models, to gain its ends and secure its purposes, than it does to the power of God through His Holy Spirit. And, it is fundamentalistic in its attitude and often McCarthyish in its tactics, when challenged by a theology that is more in line with the historical faith. In practice, it is prone to brand as simplistic, fundamentalistic, irrational, and antiprogressive or reactionary any expression of the faith that is in contradiction to its own position. This is a fundamentalistic attitude—anything which does not agree with its own more secular and deterministic view of mankind and culture in general is illogical and to be discarded as a throwback to the unenlightened past. I will deal more with the political reality of this mind-set in the structure of the church in a later chapter. Now, I want to get back to my own basic understanding of what it means to believe in Jesus Christ.

Since I was raised by a West Texas rancher father who taught his sons to pull themselves up by their own bootstraps, and that they could be what they wanted to be if they worked and tried hard enough, it has not been easy for me to accept the necessity of God's intervention in my life to set it straight. My generation was raised in the era of the "self-made man" and the popular acceptance of success symbolized by Horatio Alger. For much of the last century we have been moving toward the deification of man and the humanization of God, not only in the area of religion, but also in the areas of psychology and sociology as well. In modern times the deification of man reached its apex in Hitler and the Third Reich, and the humanization of God reached its nadir in the death-of-God theology. Much of the theology written and taught in this century denies anything that transcends our own experience and cannot be proved by rationalistic logic or empirical data. This denial has certainly included any practical belief in a transcendent God. Along with the denial of the transcendent has been the development of relativism and the eclipse of universal truth. No one has stated the fallacy and danger of such false logic better than Richard Weaver.

The denial of universals carries with it the denial of everything transcending experience. The denial of everything transcending experience means inevitably—though ways are found to hedge on this—the denial of truth. With the denial of objective truth there is no escape from the relativism of "man the measure of all things." Weaver goes on to say that when man began to see himself as "the measure of all thing," he was cut off from reality. Thus began the "abomination of desolation" appearing today as a feeling of alienation from all fixed truth.[1]

Naturally, if all of life is relativized with man at the center of things, then to talk about Incarnation, or God taking the form of a human being is either mythological or nonsense. Most Christian theologians have not been willing to label the Incarnation nonsense, but that is what they actually mean when they talk about the myth of Jesus Christ. That is, the biblical witness to Jesus Christ, in their view, is not meant to be taken as making sense in any literal fashion as a historical act of God in the course of history. If there is no transcendent God, the Creator of heaven and earth, who is totally other, then of course that God cannot reveal His nature by coming to the earth in the form of a man. And so some theologians of this century have repeated the Docetist heresy of the first century. Whoever, or whatever, God is, it could only appear that He was a man. Therefore, we must talk of the myth of God, or speak of God as mythologically revealing Himself in Incarnation; that is a way of stating a truth about deity which is not historically and actually true.

Another way around the scandal of the Incarnation is to take the position that either Jesus misinterpreted Himself as God incarnate, or that the disciples and authors of the New Testament created the kerygmatic Christ, who in reality transcended the earthly Jesus. Those having this view hold that of course Jesus Christ actually lived and was one of the great moral teachers of all times. His teachings are among the greatest in history, and we should look to Him and His teachings as a classic example of the good. C. S. Lewis in his own inimical and pungent way puts this position to rest.

I'm trying here to prevent anyone from saying the really silly thing that people often say about Him: "I'm ready to accept Jesus as a great moral teacher but I don't accept his claim to be God!" That's the one thing we mustn't say. A man who was merely a man and said the sort of things Jesus said wouldn't be a great moral teacher. He'd either be a lunatic—on a level with the man who says he's a poached egg—or else he'd be the devil of Hell. You must make your choice. Either this man was, and is, the Son of God: or else a madman or something worse. You can kill Him as a demon; or you can fall at His feet and call Him Lord and God. But don't let us come with any patronizing nonsense about His being a great human teacher. He hasn't left that open to us, and He didn't intend to.[2]

No, it doesn't make sense for us to claim to be Christians at all, unless in Jesus Christ we are dealing with God Himself and what He has revealed about Himself.

In my own experience, as I sought to come to some meaningful understanding of God, it was Jesus Christ who made God real to me. As I tried to think about, or come to terms with, the idea or reality of God, there was no place where I could take hold or find any certitude. Dean Hawk's two statements, "Jesus Christ is the key to understanding history," and, "You will never know who you are until you know Jesus Christ," caused me to look with some degree of intensity and yearning at the portrait of Jesus Christ as recorded in the Scriptures. It was there that I began to have a "sense" of myself and a "sense" of God that spoke to my mind and heart.

Dr. E. Stanley Jones speaks of the "God become intimate":

Apart from Christ we know little about God. If we try to start from God we do not start from God, but from our ideas about God. But our ideas about God are not God. We must start from God's idea about Himself, and God's idea about Himself is Christ. Jesus is God breaking through to us. He is the great simplification—God speaking to us in the only language we can understand, a human language; showing us His life in the only way we could grasp it, a human life; uncovering His character in the place where your character and mine are wrought out, a human character. Jesus is the human life of God. He is the God become intimate.

This one who is the human life of God, led me to a God whom I could know and love. As I read the New Testament, the person of Jesus Christ began to come alive for me. In the parables, the Sermon on the Mount, and the teaching of Paul about the fatal flaw in humanity which causes us to live selfish lives—hurting others and being hurt by them—I sensed a new possibility for my life. I came to the place where I was willing to begin the journey of faith by trusting that the New Testament witness to Jesus Christ was true. Perhaps Jesus Christ could heal the hurt in my own life, and perfect the flaw in me, so I could live differently in relation to God and to all the others in my life. This Jesus, His life and teaching, led me to understand and accept God's forgiveness and healing for my own life. This in turn, enabled me for the first time, to have a sense of God that was real in my life—a God who was my Father, because He was the Father of my new redeeming friend and Lord, even Jesus Christ.

It is not my purpose to write a systematic treatise about Christology or a theology of the Trinity. But, it is my purpose to speak what I believe to be the mind of Christ about Himself and the church into which He calls us as His disciples. Without Jesus Christ as Savior and Redeemer, Teacher and Master, Lord and King, there is no church—and there will be no liberation of the church for witness and ministry. It is my conviction that much of the church has ceased to preach Jesus Christ in His fullness; we have come to depend on a humanized gospel which will increasingly fail not only the church and its members, but more disastrously will fail to bring a meaningful and liberating gospel to a world lost in pleasure and hedonism, greed and avarice, injustice and intolerance, hunger and woe, and plain old sin. Surely it will require more than we have to offer from within ourselves, if we are to find purpose and meaning for our personal lives, and justice and mercy for society as a whole. If we are to be liberated for mission and ministry, we must hold up Jesus Christ as the way to authentic Christian faith. We truly drift astray when we stray from God Incarnate in Jesus Christ.

Thomas Oden in his excellent book, *Agenda for Theology*, has stated the primacy of Christ most effectively.

II

To Experience God

"I will not leave you as orphans; I will come to you. . . . If anyone loves me, he will keep My word; and My Father will love him, and We will come to him, and make Our abode with him." *(John 14:18, 23)*

He commanded them not to leave Jerusalem, but to wait for what the Father had promised, "Which," He said, "you heard from Me. . . ." "You shall receive power when the Holy Spirit has come upon you; and you shall be My witnesses both in Jerusalem, and in all Judea and Samaria, and even to the remotest part of the earth." *(Acts 1:4, 8)*

One of the significant phenomena in the life of the church during this century has been the birth and growth of the Pentecostal denominations and the charismatic movement. For much of the church during the first half of the twentieth century, this movement was looked on as sectarian, and as a fringe segment of the Christian community. Most of the leaders and members of mainline Christianity thought of

Pentecostalism as being fanatical, a kind of sentimental and emotional experience which appealed primarily to the uneducated and lower class of society. In most theological and academic circles, Pentecostalism had perhaps less credence than even fundamentalism. This judgment, and judgment it was, included educational and social class prejudice and bespoke as much about the ones making the judgment as about the Pentecostals, whom they were consigning to the fringe of the Christian church. It is a paradox that modern liberal theology has rightly taught that God has a special concern for the poor and those of lesser social and class distinction, yet has not perceived the possibility that God works in the Pentecostal movement to bring His good news of salvation and power for witness and ministry to that very segment of His people who are not being ministered to by the mainline institutional church, including the theological academies.

As theological study in the mainline traditions became more and more rationalistic and scientific in its approach, it tended to judge condescendingly Pentecostalism on the one hand, and evangelical orthodoxy on the other, as being anti-intellectual and highly emotional—even sentimental—expressions of the Christian faith. At the same time, there seemed to be a continued and growing interest across a broad cross section of society in both the Pentecostal experience and the historical orthodox faith. This was especially true in so-called Third World or undeveloped nations. In many countries of South America, Africa, and Asia, the vibrantly alive and growing church, often with a sensitive and activistic social conscience, was both Pentecostal and evangelical.

A classic example of this is the story of the Methodist Church in Chile. Early in this century a Methodist missionary in Valparaiso, Willis C. Hoover, was deeply touched by the movement of the Holy Spirit in his life and in his congregation. Attendance at worship began to increase, many conversions occurred, and the church began to grow dramatically. There were many manifestations of the presence of the power of the Holy Spirit. Charges were brought against Hoover that he was doing things that were "anti-Biblical and anti-Methodist." One result was that he was forced out of the mission movement of The Methodist Church. Another was the beginning of the Methodist Pentecostal Church in Chile. C. Peter Wagner reports:

Undaunted Hoover started separate services in 1910 and founded the Methodist Pentecostal Church. The growth of this Church through the years has been phenomenal. Some estimates put its membership at around 750,000 today. This compares with about 4,000 in the Methodist Church that did not have a place for such workings of the Holy Spirit back in 1910.[1]

This story of phenomenal growth and vitality in the Pentecostal movement in Brazil, Argentina, and other Central and South American countries is the story of the church vibrant and alive, touching the masses with the message of Christ. In many ways the attitude of mainline church leaders in the mission offices in New York is one of condescension and paternalism toward the Pentecostal movement in South America. The church there is charged with being socially and politically insensitive and not in conformity with the movement of history. And then, of course, according to them, it is just not part of "our tradition."

But, something else happened; this movement of the Holy Spirit—Pentecostal, charismatic, or neo-Pentecostal—call it what you may—began to break into mainline Christianity. By and large, the response of the mainline denominations to this breakthrough has been negative and unresponsive. While this has been especially so in many of the more orthodox or fundamental denominations, it has been surprisingly so, also, in the churches of the Wesleyan tradition, including my own denomination, The United Methodist Church. Such has not been the case with the Roman Catholic Church, which has sought to affirm the charismatic movement as a gift of God for the renewal of the church. The papacy has given encouragement to the movement and instructed the hierarchy to give it both support and guidance. This is indeed irony, that the Roman Catholic Church, which has been judged by much of Protestantism to be locked into a closed system of doctrine and polity, would be more open and inclusive toward the charismatic movement than "so-called" liberal Protestantism. Are we so locked into liberal theology—a theology tending more and more toward a secular and humanistic understanding of creation—that we really are intolerant in attitude toward other options in theology and Christian experience?

Common enemies make strange bedfellows.

For significantly different reasons than church leaders, a majority of laity are also basically suspicious and not open to charismatic renewal. I believe I am an accurate judge of the basic theology of the vast majority of the membership of our denomination when I say that they are essentially orthodox in a primitive fashion. Most of the laity, as I have come to know them, have not been won over to a demythologized secular view of the gospel. Yet, they tend to have a simplistic understanding of the Scriptures; that is, they have not studied the Scriptures and most of them have not been radically confronted with the claims of the gospel. By and large, theirs is an acculturated faith, which is more a civil religion than it is a valid experience of the person and teaching of Jesus Christ. Such "so-called" Christians want to "go to church" and be respectable citizens in the community more than "to be the church." They would prefer not to have their emotions disturbed and certainly not to have their consciences pricked. I do not say this pejoratively or with any sense of satisfaction, but with a deep concern and empathy. Unless the average congregation is carefully nurtured in the whole of biblical faith, it is seldom open either to the gift of the Holy Spirit, or to the gifts of the Spirit, and is encouraged by many church leaders and theologians to stay closed. In essence, I am affirming that the average church member is not open to the infilling of the Holy Spirit, especially to the extraordinary gifts. This should not be strange, as the pulpit has more often than not been silent, or has expressed grave reservations and criticism when the subject is discussed.

Nevertheless, the experience of the Holy Spirit and the receiving of some of the gifts keep recurring. When part of a congregation becomes open to the infilling of the Holy Spirit and to receiving the Spirit's gifts, a division often occurs in the life of the church. The charismatic movement is most often blamed for this. It is my observation, however, that a significant reason for the division rests with the main body of members in the church who want to keep things as they are. They are afraid of expressing their emotions with any enthusiasm in matters of faith. If being open to the Holy Spirit means in any way losing control of their wills and/or direction of their lives, then they are not open to the Holy Spirit. Could it be that they have never been truly open to God's salvation and direction in their lives?

At the same time, I am aware, both as a pastor and as a former district superintendent and general board executive of the church, that the Pentecostal or charismatic experience in the life of a church often brings division, usually caused by excesses in witness and experience, as well as a misunderstanding of Scripture about the gift and gifts of the Spirit. In fact, I am convinced that the overemphasis given by Pentecostalism on the extraordinary gifts of healing and speaking in tongues is not in accordance with the teaching of Scripture. It seems clear to me that Scripture does not teach that speaking in tongues is the definitive witness of the baptism or infilling of the Holy Spirit in the life of a disciple. At the same time, I do believe that Pentecostalism has been more in accord with the teaching of Scripture than has much of the established church. The mainline Protestant churches have primarily ignored the teaching of the Scripture concerning the gift of the Holy Spirit and the necessity of the Christian to receive the gifts of the Spirit in order to be properly equipped for witness and ministry.

Jesus clearly teaches that the Heavenly Father will "give the Holy Spirit to those who ask Him" (Luke 11:13). His last word to His disciples directed them to wait for the coming of the Holy Spirit. Paul clearly teaches the necessity of a believer's having the Holy Spirit. "No one can say, 'Jesus is Lord,' except by the Holy Spirit" (I Cor. 12:3). God wants to give the gifts of the Holy Spirit to the disciples of Jesus Christ; but, Paul says the Spirit decides which gifts He will bestow on each individual. "But one and the same Spirit works all these things, distributing to each one individually just as He wills" (I Cor. 12:11). While Pentecostalism may have erred in its teaching that speaking in tongues is the definitive sign of the baptism or infilling of the Holy Spirit, the rest of the church has erred more grievously in ignoring or denying the teaching of Scripture about the gift of the Holy Spirit and the gifts of the Spirit. The church of Jesus Christ, if it is the church at all, is gifted by the presence of the Holy Spirit and equipped with the gifts of the Spirit.

Many of the bishops and other leaders of our denomination have been either benignly neutral or ardently opposed to the renewal offered by the charismatic movement. They are essentially making the same error made by the bishops and leaders of the Church of England when they were not open to the renewal of the church in their day that was offered by the Wesleys. It is with deep conviction and what I discern to be the leading of the Holy Spirit in my own life, that I challenge all our leaders, especially the bishops of our church, to prayerfully look at the teaching of the Holy Scripture about the gift of the Spirit and the gifts of the Spirit.

It is clear to me that the only model offered in the Bible for the life of a disciple and for the liberation and empowerment of the church for witness and ministry is the charismatic model. In his recent book, *The Problem of Wineskins,* Howard A. Snyder, formerly dean of the Free Methodist Theological Seminary in São Paulo, Brazil, discusses at length both the biblical foundation and the practical application of the charismatic model in the quest for authentic discipleship and renewal of the church in today's world. I encourage anyone who is open to the possibility of charismatic renewal to read the whole book. (If the thought bothers you, I encourage you to go back and read again those passages from Paul in Romans, Corinthians, and Ephesians that discuss the gift of the Spirit and the gifts of the Spirit.) In his chapter "Church and Culture," Snyder says:

> In the biblical view, God gives his gracious gift of salvation on the basis of Christ's work and through the agency of the Holy Spirit. This provides the basis of the church's community life. The pure light of God's "manifold grace" is then refracted as it shines through the church, producing the varied, many-colored charismata. This provides the basis for the church's diversity within unity. The church is edified through the exercise of spiritual gifts as "the whole body, joined and knit together by every joint with which it is supplied, . . . makes bodily growth and upbuilds itself in love" (Eph. 4:16).
> This is important in order to have a healthy, growing church. In order for the church to reach its true, biblical potential, it must be based on a charismatic model, not an institutional model. Churches which structure themselves charismatically are largely prepared for the future. But churches which are encased in rigid, bureaucratic, institutional structures may soon find themselves trapped in culturally bound forms which are fast becoming obsolete.[2]

If the Spirit of Christ is not in us, and if His gifts do not equip and empower us, then we are left on our own without any help beyond ourselves to try to live the life of Jesus Christ. And, because we have tried—when we have tried at all—to live the Christian life on our own, we have failed miserably to touch modern secular humanity for Christ. Either as modern paternalistic liberals or, often, as pharisaical legalists we have reflected too little love and attractiveness in our lives.

It is not necessary that this be so. Through faith in Jesus Christ, we can experience God's forgiveness of our sin, His rescue from our rebellion, and His reconciliation in His love. As we receive His reconciling love and open our lives to His Spirit, He begins His work of healing and mercy in our lives. The reconciling which is begun in Jesus Christ restores us to our Father God in a love-love relationship from a love-hate relationship, and is then spread to and through our relationships in our families and in all our social relationships. But, this is not something that we must accomplish on our own. God wants to work in us through the Spirit, as promised by Jesus, to equip us to live the life and faith of Jesus Christ through the fruit and gifts of the Holy Spirit. None of this is possible, no matter how noble may be our intentions or how ardently we may strive, without the gift of God's Holy Spirit and the equipping through His gifts for a life of discipleship.

Though there is some lukewarm affirmation of the charismatic experience as valid in the life of the church, no prophetic voice has been raised in strong support of a movement which is clearly having an impact on the life of the church for the overall good. In fact, I personally know of many leaders of the church who are covertly opposed to the movement and who will never knowingly advance a pastor who is openly a part of the charismatic renewal. I know some of our leading bishops who have stated that such pastors are not needed in the Methodist tradition. I am sure that a like-minded Anglican bishop said of John and Charles Wesley, "We don't need men like the Wesleys in the Anglican tradition." It seems to me that history has vindicated the life and the ministry of the Wesleys, as I am convinced that contemporary church history will attest to the positive influence of charismatic renewal.

As a United Methodist pastor, I have covenanted to be a faithful disciple of Jesus Christ. I have been called to teach and preach the word, to administer the sacraments of the church, and to be a faithful pastor. Experience has taught me, through God's merciful grace and His love, that I do not have the natural talents or abilities to be faithful to the covenant which I have made. If I am to preach, it will be in the power of the Holy Spirit and through the gift of preaching. If I am to teach, it will be by the Holy Spirit and through the gift of teaching. If I am to be a faithful priest in sharing in His sacramental grace, it will be through being open to the Holy Spirit. If I am to have the wisdom, discernment, and proper leadership as a pastor, it will be in the Holy Spirit and through the gift of pastoral insight. It is not self-righteous but God-affirming to confess that to whatever extent I have faithfully fulfilled my covenant with God, it has been through the gift of His Spirit and the gifts of His Spirit in and to my life. And that is all that it means—but it means all that—that living victoriously as a child of God, and especially for one who ministers in a church for God, can only be done through the indwelling of the Holy Spirit, through faith in Jesus Christ, and through the gifts of the Spirit. To be Christian at all is to have the Spirit of God—and to be able to live effectively as a serving disciple of God is to have the gifts of the Holy Spirit. Again, the only biblical model for the life of a Christian or of the church is the charismatic model. This is the clear teaching of the Scripture which is the primary foundation for faith and practice. I am convinced that life in and of the Holy Spirit is affirmed as the only valid Christian experience and is part of our tradition when properly understood.

I do not intend in this book to give any detailed teaching on the whole theology of the Holy Spirit or of the theology of gifts. There are many such books available from within the Pentecostal tradition, from the other Protestant traditions, as well as from the Roman Catholic Church. It has been my clear intention to call to the attention of the church my deep conviction, which I discern to be the leading of His Spirit, that we have erred as leaders and as a church where we have not welcomed the charismatic movement and directed its course within the church, through clear Scriptural teaching. I am convinced, also, that this is a primary responsibility of the episcopal office.

It is a primary function and responsibility of the pastoral office to teach the faith. If bishops and other church leaders will give pastoral leadership to a theology of the Holy Spirit and the gifts of the Spirit, they will be a part of the liberation of the church for witness and ministry in our day.

III

God's Clear Call

Now the Lord said to Abram,
"Go forth from your country,
And from your relatives
And from your father's house,
To the land which I will show you;
And I will make you a great nation,
And I will bless you,
And make your name great;
And so you shall be a blessing;
And I will bless those who bless you,
And the one who curses you I will curse.
And in you all the families of the earth shall be blessed."
So Abram went forth as the Lord had spoken to him.

(Gen. 12:1-4a)

To know Jesus Christ, to truly know Him both as Savior and Lord, and through this trusting faith to experience God Himself as the Holy Spirit, brings a clear and all encompassing call. The call of God which came to Abraham is renewed again and again in each generation, and now comes to each of us. We are to respond in faithful obedience so that we might receive God's blessing. But, the call and the blessing are not a "privilege"! No, we retain that blessing and its benefits to us only as we are willing to be a blessing to others. This is both a particular and an all-inclusive invitation of God to place our lives in His hands, under His direction, in a kind of trusting faith, in the face of our doubts and fears and despite any apparent human contradictions and/or impossibilities with which we may be faced.

On the face of it, God asked Abraham, when he was nearly ninety and Sarah well past the age of bearing children, to leave their country and go wherever God might ultimately require—with the expressed promise that the blessing of God would come through Abraham's and Sarah's own offspring. The writer of Hebrews sharpens the faith and obedience of Abraham when he says: "By faith Abraham, when he was called, obeyed by going out to a place which he was to receive for an inheritance; and he went out, not knowing where he was going" (Heb. 11:8). This call and response of Abraham is the prototype, along with the life and teaching of Jesus Christ, for the one in all succeeding generations who wants to be a faithful child of God. I make much of it here because I am convinced that a like response on the part of Christians today is absolutely essential to the liberation of the church for witness and ministry. We are called to an understanding of life where God and His providential love are at the center of all that we are and do. It is just possible that modern secular humanity may be able, through God's seeking Spirit and grace, to truly hear this call of God today. Humanity's despair, alienation, and loss of confidence make it impossible to build a good world through its own efforts, and without faith in a living God.

In previous chapters I have attempted to present the necessity of taking seriously the claims of Jesus Christ about Himself and His work as Savior and Redeemer of a lost humanity if we are to have renewal of faith and valid

Christian experience in the church today. Also, I have stated that this experience of God is made real in our lives through the indwelling of the Holy Spirit in our hearts as a result of our obedient faith and trust in Jesus Christ. Not only is God willing to give us the gift of His Spirit, through faith in Christ, but also He will equip and empower us with the capability to live as effective and positive servant-disciples in touching the lives of others and meeting their needs. Clearly, it is impossible to know and acknowledge Jesus as Savior and Lord without the Holy Spirit, just as it is impossible to live an authentic Christian life without the gift of the Spirit and the use of the gifts of the Spirit for service and ministry to others.

If what I have said in the preceding paragraph is true, and I believe it is, why is it so hard for us to live our lives in the pattern of the faith of Abraham and after the example of Jesus Christ? Even serious Christians both liberal and evangelical, and certainly nominal institutional Christians of either parentage, give more evidence of failure than success as examples of a Christlike witness to God and His saving love for all of us. One of the primary reasons for the rejection of a living Christian faith by many people is a false psychological self-understanding which has been generally accepted in society today.

Paul C. Vitz writes perceptively about this in his recent book, *Psychology as Religion: The Cult of Self-Worship.*[1] It is the contention of Vitz, and I think rightly, that much of modern psychology has adopted a view of humanity that sees the human self as the center of reality and meaning with an innate nature that tends toward good rather than toward evil. This false and ultimately destructive view of humanity has been substituted for the orthodox Christian understanding of human beings as creatures of God, who have through the sin of rebellion and pride disobeyed God and attempted to assume sole responsibility for guiding and directing their own destinies. After all, if we naturally tend to be good and unselfish, that is, if we naturally love our neighbors as ourselves, then there is no rational reason why we cannot be right, do right, and build a good world. For those who really want to be rational, however, the question, Why are we failing so miserably in building that good world? must surely come.

It is interesting to note that Vitz witnesses to the abandonment of what he terms a nominal Christian upbringing to become a teacher and exponent of a psychology of humanity which has both secular and humanistic characteristics in its foundations. As he studied and taught in the discipline of psychology, he developed, he says, "a growing awareness that I found much humanistic personality theory false and rather silly . . . I still remember moments in the middle of class lectures when I suddenly became aware that I was saying things which I didn't believe."[2] It was during this time that Professor Vitz became a professing Christian. About his adult conversion to the Christian faith, which he had previously abandoned, he writes: "There is nothing dramatic to report about the latter—no sudden rebirth or mystical experience—just a great deal of intense emotional turbulence associated with the collapse of my secular ideals accompanied by a quietly growing change of heart and mind. This process seems to have started sometime in 1972, and at some point since then I discovered I was a Christian—a very poor one to be sure, but still my life had been turned around."[3] It is Vitz's thesis that "psychology has become a religion, in particular a form of secular humanism based on the worship of the self."[4] Certainly, it should be apparent that such psychological understanding of humanity is patently unchristian or as Vitz puts it,

It should be obvious—though it has apparently not been so to many—that the relentless and single-minded search for and glorification of the self is at direct cross purposes with the Christian injunction to lose the self. Certainly Jesus neither lived nor advocated a life that would qualify by today's standards as "self-actualized." For the Christian the self is the problem, not the potential paradise. Understanding this problem involves an awareness of sin, especially of the sin of pride; correcting this condition requires the practice of such unself-actualized states as contrition and penitence, humility, obedience, and trust in God.[5]

Such a secular and humanistic understanding of humanity from a psychological standpoint seems to parallel the theological humanization of God and the deification of the human being in recent years. If from both a theological and a psychological understanding of the race, humanity, as species and as individual, is the supreme being and therefore has within the self all the answers about existence that are needed, then it becomes a natural result that one should worship the self. Also, it is the obvious conclusion with such a self-understanding that whatever salvation or fulfillment we are to have will come as a result of our own efforts. With the breakthroughs in science and technology it is no wonder then that we began to see a perfected humanity and the continued improvement in the social order. Humanity really began to believe that we could build the "kingdom of God on earth," i.e., "The Great Society" and other messianic socio-political terms. In other words, the modern "tree of knowledge," science and technology, has truly freed humans so they can determine their own destiny and perfect their society. It seems as if modern man, in every age, is destined to commit again the original sin of Adam.

The consumer-pleasure-oriented society is also a natural outgrowth of such theology and psychology. If we ourselves are our own ends, then it follows that it is right and good to sate our appetites and gorge our pleasures. The acute problem with all this is that it creates a society of greed and sin, of alienation and conflict, of loneliness and death. Instead of creating a world where all our problems are solved, we are confronted with an ever-more complex world with mounting social and economic problems and the recurring evil of humanity's inhumanity toward itself. This inhumanity is reflected in such events as the Great Depression, World War II, Dachau and Buchenwald, the threat of a nuclear holocaust, hunger and famine throughout much of the so-called "Third World," Pol Pot and Cambodia, the tyranny of totalitarianism both of the left and of the right, the systematic persecution of the Christian Church especially in Marxist countries, the evolvement of the permissive society with the breakdown in the family structure and the erosion of any standards in morality, the increasing dependence on drugs for meaning in life with the accompanying despair and alienation from the rest of society, and on and on. In worshiping ourselves, we incarnate sin or self-pride at the center of our existence and face the inevitable end—life without meaning and death without hope.

In the face of this, it is indeed encouraging to me that prophetic voices from within the realm of science are calling us back to a theological understanding of humanity which is much more consistent with the biblical picture. Russell Kirk in *Enemies of the Permanent Things* quotes Dr. Edmund W. Sinnot, then dean of the graduate school of Yale University, who wrote in *The Bulletin of the Atomic Scientists*, December 1960:

The days of the evolutionary optimist, are gone . . . who believed that progress is inherent in the nature of things and that man is bound to grow better almost automatically. If we are to find our way out of our troubles, we must appeal not only to the rational attitudes and methods of the scientist but also to man's inner spiritual motivation. Love may turn out to be a more valuable resource than logic.

For Sinnot science cannot supplant religion; both science and religion "have indispensible contributions to make to the great task of building a society in which man will not only be safe and wise and happy and loving, but will gain the serene confidence that their lives are in harmony with the universe itself."[6]

In a time such as we live in now, where despair has become the norm of life for many, and where we are perhaps facing more realistically our own limitations, is it possibly the time when the message of faith in the living God can be heard again? I believe that it is.

Within the church today are at least three groups of people who claim to be Christians but who have not truly heard the gospel in its all encompassing and inclusive requirements. These three, along with those nontheistic secularists outside the church, all comprise "the fields, that . . . are white for harvest" for the teaching and preaching of the gospel. Quite often, the "whole" gospel is more offensive and is resisted more strongly by those partial Christians within the church than by those who have chosen consciously or unconsciously to live outside the authentic faith. Let us look now at those general groups within the church who have at best a limited or partial understanding of Christian discipleship.

The largest group of church members who have not heard the call of God that Abraham heard and that Jesus incarnated, and who therefore are not good witnesses for Jesus Christ, are what we might call nominal Christians, those who are "lukewarm" in their faith. Most of these observe a kind of "civil religion" or acculturated faith as their nominal relationship to Jesus Christ and His church. They have been greatly and significantly influenced by the secular-humanist view of psychology and humanity. They seem to sense the desirability, if not need, to keep some attachment to the traditions of faith, but not to all the practices of faith. While they continue to go to church with somewhat regular participation in worship services, the determining decisions of their lives, as they understand them, are controlled by economic, social, and political forces. In other words, while they still tip their hats on Sundays to the God of history, their real gods are success, money, social status, and standing—those realities of life which enable self-love and self-gratification. This group is by far the largest and most difficult to reach with the total claims of the gospel. Here, in reality, is the core weakness of the modern church. These comfortable church members who are trying to live respectably in two worlds, and not being true to the values of either, must be afflicted with the judgment of the gospel.

There are two other general groups within the church who take seriously the claims of the Christian faith but who have a very limited and faulty understanding of what it means to be a disciple of Jesus Christ. These groups are generally ardently, and often stridently, opposed to each other, and tend to classify each other as outside the authentic Christian faith. Each is guilty of building walls of separation instead of bridges of understanding. I speak, of course, of those who are advocates and proponents of the "personal gospel" of salvation and eternal life, who believe that the Christian faith is right belief and personal experience and that there is no such thing as an authentic "social gospel." On the other hand, others think the authentic Christian faith is the "social gospel"; they think it is not as important what we believe, as it is what we do with our lives in helping meet the needs of others, especially the poor and the oppressed.

The first group places great emphasis on right belief about God and Jesus Christ and on what God has specifically done to save us from our sins in the Incarnation—the birth, life, death, and resurrection of Jesus Christ. The primary ethical implication of the faith for such people has to do with personal morality and is individualistic in its implications. Surely, it is at best a half gospel. Opposed to this partial and limited understanding of the Christian faith is the second group, the advocates of the so-called "social gospel." For these the teachings of Jesus Christ have importance, especially the words of Jesus in Matthew 25 where the description of the last judgment is found. According to the "social gospel," the true disciples of our Lord are those who have fed the hungry, clothed the naked, given hospitality to the stranger, and visited those in prison. In other words authentic Christian faith is to be found in those who do the "good works" of the kingdom. Proponents of the "social gospel" use Matthew 25 in a proof text like the evangelical traditionalists stress salvation from sin and justification by faith alone. Just as surely as the advocates of the "personal gospel" teach and live out, at best, a half gospel, those advocates of the "social gospel" are equally guilty of misunderstanding the Christian faith and misrepresenting it in what they teach. Such an expression of the faith is far more true to a "secular humanistic" understanding of humanity than it is to the traditional Christian view of a humanity marred by selfishness and pride, in need of forgiveness and reconciliation, in order that the life-changing love of one's neighbor might replace the "self-actualization" of pride of self.

I am attempting to say in this book that the artificial and man-erected walls have separated the gospel into personal and social, and must be torn down if the church is to be liberated for witness and ministry. I am well aware that lip service has been given to this great need, but I am equally convinced that the primary division is still there and has yet to be bridged or healed.

Richard F. Lovelace suggests that Jesus was speaking to this very issue when He warned, "Beware of the leaven of the Pharisees and Sadducees" (Matt. 16:6).

Jesus warned the disciples to beware of the leaven of the Pharisees and Sadducees, that is, the conservatives and the liberals. Both of these groups—in other words, all of us—have a hidden gravity toward error and a way of adding and subtracting to the Biblical revelation which results in teaching for doctrine the precepts of men.[7]

It has been relatively easy for modern liberals to make the pejorative label of "Pharisee" stick to the more evangelical or fundamental Christians, sometimes with legitimate cause. But Jesus said, "Beware of the Sadducees," also. One aspect of His warning must have included His rejection of the basic stance of the Sadducees—that the doing of good or evil rested solely in the free will of man—in other words, that by his own efforts without God's provident intervention within his personal life he could right the evil in the world.

For some this may seem too simplistic an interpretation of the warning of Jesus, but I am convinced that the point I am making is included in what Jesus said. Let me be more explicit. The Pharisees were the interpreters of the Jewish law and the keepers of right doctrine and faith in the Hebrew tradition. They attempted to live strictly in fulfillment of the law, and though many were self-righteous and hypocritical, at least some tried to live and teach a true piety in worship of God and in all daily living. It would be fair to conclude, though, that Pharisaism was more judgmental than forgiving, and more rigid in its religious demands than it was loving in its relationships. It is the pejorative charge of Pharisaism that has been made against much of the so-called evangelical or orthodox Christianity in our day. As I have indicated before, to some extent, this charge is true—especially where the evangelical or orthodox faith has insisted on right doctrine at the expense of concerned and caring love expressed in our daily lives.

But, let me point out again that Jesus said, "Beware of the leaven of the Sadducees" as well as that of the Pharisees. This has not been as readily understood as an equally grave error that is expressed in a segment of the church today. In general the Sadducees were conservative aristocrats concerned with maintaining the status quo. In this they are like many middle-class acculturated Christians committed to civil religion. In other ways, however, they were quite similar to modern liberal secular humanists. They denied the existence of angels and spirits, taught that the destiny of humanity resided in itself—without the need of divine providence—and believed that the determination of good and evil was directed by their own free wills. It is in this sense that they are like modern secularist man who may, or may not, still tip his hat to a traditional concept of God, but actually affirms that his own ultimate reality and destiny rests in himself. This attitude is the fatal flaw in much of modern liberal Christianity with all of its valid concern for meeting the needs of others. The person who does not acknowledge basic human sin and the need for personal redemption and salvation through God's atonement for his or her sin in Jesus Christ has not understood the gospel at all in a holistic sense.

It has been my observation that there is no lasting power of motivation for witness and ministry without acknowledging and receiving the presence and power of the Holy Spirit through faith in Jesus Christ. When church members, or adherents to the Christian tradition, leave off the personal and spiritual experience of salvation in and through Jesus Christ, they are unable to lead others into Christian service and ministry. Also, many talk more about their social concern and commitment than they actually risk in personal encounter by investing their lives. At the same time, when the more liberal and secularly inclined pastors and laypersons show a real concern and involvement in ministering to the needs of others, we who are more evangelical in our orientation should not hesitate to join hands with them in doing all the good we can. Frankly, I am more comfortable with such concerned and involved liberals, than I am with traditionally orthodox church members, who practice faith primarily by going to church, but do not give themselves in meeting the needs of others.

Here again, one does not have to settle with less than authentic and holistic Christian commitment. Much of the so-called evangelical community within the established church today is willing to acknowledge that it has failed to profess and live out a balanced Christian faith. Too often, evangelicals have failed to invest their lives in Christlike commitment in loving and serving their neighbor. Certainly, I join in confessing my own failure to risk and give my life as I always should in daily living; but, this in no way indicates that I then commit myself to any theology or psychology of humanity which does not acknowledge my own need for forgiveness and reconciliation through a personal experience of God's love in Jesus Christ. In fact, my own unwillingness to give my life in witness and ministry, as Jesus Christ gave His life for others, is proof of my own sin and need for healing through the grace and mercy of God. It is my earnest prayer and hope that those who are turned off by a more orthodox expression of the Christian faith, yet see themselves as Christians in a social and mission sense, will also come to see that they are in error when they rule out rebirth and regeneration and the absolute need for the Living Christ as the key to liberation for witness and ministry.

When more and more evangelically oriented Christians see the imperative for the social expression of the Christian faith and when more and more liberal and secularly oriented Christians see the need for confessing personal sin and for personal redemption in their lives, the church can then be liberated for witness and ministry. When these two segments of modern Christianity see their need for each other in order for either to be whole, then the church will reclaim its wholeness. And, perhaps, as we speak with a common witness and ministry, many in the world today will respond to the claims of Jesus Christ in their lives. We desperately need to be liberated, from ourselves, that we might hear the clear call of God who wants to bless us and bless others through us.

IV

The Confusion of Pluralism

As to all opinions which do not strike at the root of Christianity, we think and let think. So that, whatsoever they are, whether right or wrong, they are no distinguishing marks of a Methodist. . . .

I beseech you, brethren, by the mercies of God, that we be in no wise divided among ourselves. Is thy heart right, as my heart is with thine? I ask no further question. If it be, give me thy hand. For opinions, or terms, let us not destroy the work of God. Dost thou love and serve God? It is enough. I give thee the right hand of fellowship.[1]   —*John Wesley*

One of the significant characteristics of Methodism throughout its history is that it has been catholic or inclusive in its spirit, and ecumenical or open toward other churches or denominations. We do not require rebaptism when persons from other Christian churches present themselves for membership. If you profess Jesus Christ as Savior and Lord and pledge your allegiance to His kingdom; if you profess the Christian faith as contained in the Scriptures of the Old and New Testaments; if you promise to live, by God's grace, a

Christian life and always remain a faithful member of Christ's holy church; and if you promise to uphold the church by your prayers, your presence, your gifts, and your service; then, you are accepted into the membership of the church and as a disciple of Jesus Christ.[2] This is true whether you come from the Pentecostal or Baptist traditions, or from the Anglican, or Lutheran, or Roman Catholic traditions—or some other denominational expression of traditional Christianity.

But, you may rejoin, "Does not taking those vows tie things down rather well? Is that not asking a lot for one to become a member of Christ's church? How about John Wesley's injunction to 'think and let think'?" My own answers to these questions are clear and unambiguous, as I believe John Wesley's answers were equally clear and unambiguous. Yes, to be a Christian ties things down rather well in a covenant relationship with God. The claims of Christian discipleship are all-inclusive and ask a lot of one who is truly seeking to receive Jesus Christ as Savior and to follow Him as Lord. Further, John Wesley's "think and let think" had to do only with "opinions which do not strike at the root of Christianity." That one can be a faithful member of Christ's church and choose what to believe about His divinity and humanity, that a Christian can divorce daily living from right belief, or that one can be a good Methodist without a core of Christian belief and faith as well as a commitment to holy living is nonsense—and would have been called so by John Wesley.

This is why I began this book with the statement of a basic dependence on Holy Scripture as the essential Methodist rule of "faith and practice." I then followed with the clear understanding that to be a Christian meant to know Jesus Christ as Savior and to follow Him as Lord. This experience of the saving and life-giving reality of Christ is made possible by the prevenient grace of God through His Holy Spirit. God truly seeks and chooses us before we are ever able to say yes to His choosing. We know God in and through the Holy

Spirit, and then we hear God's *clear call* to follow Him in the Abrahamic model. These essentials of the Christian faith are not, in any real measure, subject to the opinions of those who are responsible and committed disciples of Jesus Christ.

One of the real confusions of our denomination today is a misunderstanding and a misapplication of the concept of "theological pluralism" as both an acceptable and desirable characteristic of what it means to be a Christian within the Methodist tradition. This concept has been fostered as a doctrine—serving as an umbrella—which is purported in spirit at least to allow a United Methodist Christian to believe almost anything about God or Jesus Christ, while remaining true to the faith. Such a perversion of the doctrine of pluralism allows the Christian to be guided by an essentially relativistic ethic or moral ethos. The result is that moral and ethical decisions are determined by one's own freedom of conscience, without any objective standards of truth about Christian life and behavior. The very term "theological pluralism" is used to allow or condone almost any theological or ethical position—provided that position is within the psychological framework of a liberal and humanistic interpretation of faith and life. Yet, as I have previously indicated, for much of the basic leadership of the church the umbrella is not broad enough to include the "charismatic renewal" or the more "evangelical orthodox" interpretation of the faith.

It is my conviction, as I write these words, that there is a real, if not officially declared, open season on anyone who openly espouses a more orthodox or charismatic interpretation of the Christian faith in United Methodism today. I am also aware that this will be vigorously denied by the leadership of the church. It is, therefore, not without some trepidation and concern that I am following my conviction and attempting to move the dialogue into the open throughout the church. I have found that many of the leaders of modern secular liberalism do not hesitate to go to the theological jugular vein of anyone, who with some cogency and success advances the evangelical or orthodox theological understanding of the Christian faith to which I am committed. This is inevitably done by branding such a person as a "fundamentalist," a "reactionary," or as one who is either ignorant or does not think. As I have indicated before this seems to me to be a fundamentalism of liberalism that is just as judgmental and exclusivistic as any reactionary fundamentalism of the past or present. It is to be supposed that these "liberals," so-called and misnamed, would have gone for the theological scalp of Wesley, Whitefield, Asbury, and other Methodist stalwarts if they had been living in their day. This liberalism is peculiarly illiberal in attitude and practice.

When this tactic was applied to me, first while I was in seminary, I reacted in a somewhat adolescent way, for a while at least, by openly wearing the Phi Beta Kappa key which I had earned in undergraduate school. My purpose was to indicate that, while I might be untrained or even in error in my theology, I was neither dumb nor ignorant.

Within the United Methodist tradition, most of the ministers I know who are more or less evangelical, and that would include some seminary professors, have been unwilling to confront openly this falsely liberal and more secular and humanistic interpretation of the faith due to their loyalty to the church—and perhaps also due to their concern for their future career in the church. I understand this hesitant concern, for I too love the church and deeply want to be a part of the renewal of a vibrant faith within the church and have no desire or intention to foster division or discord. At the same time my ultimate loyalty is to the Lord of the church, Jesus Christ, and to the faith that has as its primary foundation the witness recorded in the Scriptures. While I plan to deal with this more in detail later, the primary heresy of our denomination today is the pragmatic insistence on loyalty to the system, rather than loyalty to any definitive statement of the faith, or even to Jesus Christ. Incidentally, it has been most difficult for me to understand why more of our evangelically inclined bishops are not willing to confront this secular and humanistic trend in the church today. After all, their future is not at stake, and I cannot believe that they are truly willing to compromise their faith in the interest of something called the "fraternity" which they share within the Council of Bishops—or even the shadowy illusion of a united church.

Certainly, anyone who reads what I have said here has the right to disagree, and even to feel perhaps that I write from a bias. It is without apology that I write from what I trust is a progressive evangelical perspective. It is also my honest conviction, as of most evangelicals whom I know, that the basic leadership of the church has a bias against the evangelical or more orthodox pastors and laity of the church, as well as a bias against those who are part of the "charismatic" renewal movement. I know many laypersons from every walk of life and from all regions of the country who identify themselves as charismatics or evangelicals and commit themselves to helping bring renewal of the church in witness and ministry. By and large, they feel "put down." Their sense is that the leadership of the church is not sympathetic to the movement of the Holy Spirit in the life of the church.

I make this plea, especially to the bishops of our church. I sincerely implore you to be as open to the position which I and millions of others represent, as you have been to those who represent what has been described as modern or liberal Christianity. Many advocates of a "so-called" liberal theology or Christianity are basically "fundamentalistic" or closed in their attitude toward evangelical or more traditionally oriented Christians. Many of us have felt, rightly or wrongly, that this includes many of the episcopal leaders of our Church. I, for one, would be very happy to have my mind changed in the future.

It was indeed encouraging to me to see the report in

Newscope dated November 21, 1980, on the statement made to the Council of Bishops by Bishop Roy C. Nichols, president of the Council. The caption for the report in *Newscope* was: PERIL OF CHURCH IS CHEAP PLURALISM, SAYS BISHOP NICHOLS.

Bishop Roy C. Nichols (New York), president of the Council of Bishops, told his colleagues that the church's "theological peril today is in the area of cheap pluralism."

Speaking to the Nov. 11-14 council meeting, Nichols said the church is "so involved in separate agendas, so forgetful of our covenantal bond within the church, nation and world that we have magnified our differences and minimized the unifying strength of our diversity." He said, "We have acted and spoken as though our pluralism permits us to pick and choose which part of the gospel we will employ and enjoy and which part we will reject and put aside. We have made large our labels . . . liberal, conservative, moral majorities and moral minorities. . . . But is Christ really that divided? . . . We have been called as a unified community of faith to save the world and not to contribute to its division."[3]

Bishop Nichols puts his finger on a basic weakness within our church at this time—the lack of a clear and unambiguous commitment and witness to the Lordship of Jesus Christ in and over our lives. This commitment and witness certainly must include the obvious necessity for individual and personal redemption for all of us from our selfishness and fallen nature; but, it must just as obviously include the reality that our lives are lived in society and that the committed Christian must always risk his or her life in confronting evil and injustice in that society. Never one or the other—always both!

Let us look further, now, at the whole question of pluralism. While it is true that John Wesley did affirm that "as to all opinions which do not strike at the root of Christianity, we think and let think" and further "for opinions, or terms, let us not destroy the work of God," it is equally true that there are a number of things which Wesley held as essential to valid doctrine and as guides for valid Christian experience. Professor Albert Outler points out:

Wesley is quite specific and quite adamant about the essential doctrines of Christianity—and quite "orthodox"! Yet his "catholic spirit" seeks to find that community of Christians which is constituted by faith and love ("'thy 'heart' as my 'heart'"), and which is a necessary precondition to the fruitful negotiation of legitimate differences of opinion and practice.[4]

For instance, within the quadrilateral that Wesley used as a guideline for theologizing—that is, Scripture, tradition, reason, and experience—he clearly put a primacy on Scripture, in a real sense giving it an importance far greater than the other three. This position is affirmed in the "Doctrinal Guidelines in The United Methodist Church" as adopted by the General Conference in Atlanta, Georgia, in 1972.

United Methodists share with all other Christians the conviction that Scripture is the primary source and guideline for doctrine.[5]

In the pamphlet, *The Character of a Methodist,* from which the quote at the beginning of this chapter is taken, Wesley makes it plain that Christians do believe certain things and live a certain way. Circumscribing his statements about opinions, Wesley states:

We believe, indeed, that 'all Scripture is given by the inspiration of God'; . . . We believe the written word of God to be the only and sufficient rule both of Christian faith and practice; . . . We believe Christ to be the eternal, supreme God.

And then only did Wesley say,

But as to all opinions which do not strike at the root of Christianity, we think and let think.

Further on Wesley asks the question,

'What then is the mark? Who is a Methodist, according to your own account?' I answer: A Methodist is one who has 'the love of God shed abroad in his heart by the Holy Ghost given unto him'; one who 'loves the Lord his God with all his heart, and with all his soul, and with all his mind, and with all his strength'.[6]

In this pamphlet, and in his sermon on the "catholic spirit," Wesley makes a clear call for the Methodist Christian to be open and charitable toward the views of others and to relate to others with an attitude of love and not one of division and judgment. At the same time, let me emphasize again that John Wesley believed in a supernatural God, the God who had revealed Himself in His Son, Jesus Christ who was crucified for us. He required that the eye of a Christian be "single," always fixed on Jesus Christ. Methodists are to have a holy "reverence" for God and to love God and their neighbor in "affection" and in "good works." Methodists are to pray—for themselves and for others including their enemies. And, Methodists are to exhibit a catholic spirit toward those of different opinions. But, said Wesley:

A catholic spirit . . . is not an indifference to all opinions. This is the spawn of hell, not the offspring of heaven. This unsettledness of thought, this being "driven to and fro and tossed about with every wind of doctrine" [cf. Eph. 4:14], is a great curse, not a blessing; an irreconcilable enemy, not a friend, to true catholicism. A man of a truly catholic spirit has not now his religion to seek. He is fixed as the sun in his judgment concerning the main branches of Christian doctrine. It is true he is always ready to hear and weigh whatsoever can be offered against his principles. But as this does not show any wavering in his own mind, so neither does it occasion any. He does not halt between two opinions, nor vainly endeavor to blend them into one. Observe this, you who know not what spirit ye are of, who call yourselves men of the catholic spirit only because you are of a muddy understanding, because your mind is all in a mist , because you have no settled, consistent principles, but are for jumbling all opinions together. Be convinced that you have quite missed your way; you know not where you are. You think you are got into the very spirit of Christ when, in truth, you are nearer the spirit of anti-christ. Go first and learn the first elements of the gospel of Christ, and then shall you learn to be of a truly catholic spirit.[7]

It is apparent that John Wesley believed both in a "catholic spirit" and in the "essential doctrines" of the Christian faith. When it comes to matters of faith which have to do with our salvation, let us not talk about any silly and dangerous doctrine of pluralism. Using the Scripture as primary within our tradition and applying our reason along with our own Christian experience, let us be hesitant indeed to tamper with Christian orthodoxy—in doctrine or in practice. Let United Methodists again preach and teach the salvation that is offered to all through the birth, life, death, and resurrection of Jesus Christ. Let us affirm that the Holy Spirit is the One who leads us into all truth and opens the Scriptures to the eyes of faith as well as empowers our lives for witness and ministry. Let us see the Christian faith as lived out in covenant with God and with one another in and through the church. Let us teach and affirm with our lives that the Christian faith has to do with all of life—personal and social—spiritual and moral—individual and community. And, finally, let us have done with wrongly dividing the family of God into false divisions as a result of foolish or petty opinions, but let us understand clearly that certain doctrines of the church, about matters of faith and morality which we must teach and by which we must live if we are to be true to the God we serve are more dear than life to us.

V

Holiness of Heart and Life (I)

Therefore be imitators of God, as beloved children; and walk in love, just as Christ also loved you, and gave Himself up for us, an offering and a sacrifice to God as a fragrant aroma.

But do not let immorality or any impurity or greed even be named among you, as is proper among saints.

(Eph. 5:1-3)

By salvation [a Methodist] means holiness of heart and life. [1]
—*John Wesley*

There is probably no more unlikely image defining the life of a Christian for the modern church member than that of living a holy life. No one wants to be a "holy Joe," or "holy Jane," set apart from everyone else. All of us have a basic desire to be like others and to be liked by others. Notwithstanding this basic attitude, the Scriptures are clear and our tradition is centered in the pattern of holy living as the given model for the norm of the Christian life. The Christian is chosen and called to be the habitation of the Holy Spirit who comes to counsel and guide, heal and make whole, and ultimately conform our lives to the pattern of Jesus Christ, God's new beginning for humanity and the head of the church. The church of Jesus will not be liberated for witness and ministry in this or any age until the people of God aspire to and prayerfully seek to live holy lives.

Wesley speaks of holiness of heart and life. Paul admonishes the disciples of his day to be "imitators of God, as beloved children, and walk in love, just as Christ also loved you." Of course, this is where the divergence of disagreement in the church becomes evident. What does it mean to "walk in love, just as Christ also loved you"? What does it mean in social and ethical responsibility? We have previously mentioned the "personal" versus the "social" gospel. In matters of morals and ethics, we must not countenance or encourage this false division. In the Christian faith, there can be no such thing as private or personal morality apart from ethical and moral responsibility in the social realm. It is my conviction that Scripture does give us clear guidance through the written word and the teaching of the Holy Spirit so that we can make responsible decisions in both of these arenas of our lives. Also, we can look to the Wesleyan tradition for a rich heritage and teaching about holiness of heart and life.

For holiness of heart and life to have any real and substantive meaning, holiness must have a reference point. Obviously it would be highly subjective to speak of "holiness" if nothing is holy, or more important if there is not a Holy One. John Wesley had a reference point, the Holy God, the Creator and Sustainer of the universe, the Father of Abraham, Isaac, and Jacob, the One who revealed himself in these "latter days" as Jesus Christ, His Son and our Lord. We are to be "imitators of [that] God," using Jesus Christ as the model and firstborn of a new race into which we are adopted through faith. It is Jesus Christ, through the Holy Spirit, who will enable us to live holy lives.

All of us who have been ordained in The United Methodist

Church have been asked clearly to commit ourselves to holy living. Four of the first five questions which are asked the candidate for ordination have to do with living a life that is being perfected in God's love.

Are you going on to perfection?
Do you expect to be made perfect in love in this life?
Are you earnestly striving after it?
Are you resolved to devote yourself wholly to God and His work?[2]

This is clearly one of the central teachings of our tradition, that the disciple can be sanctified or made perfect in love in and through the Holy Spirit. In other words, if we are seriously to name the name of Jesus Christ as Savior and Lord, then we are to make our lives available to God, who not only will perfect us in His love, but also will guide and direct us in all things. As I understand such a faith commitment, I thereby acknowledge that I do not belong to myself but to God. Any rights or control which I thereafter exercise over my life are to be in obedience to God's will and providence for me. My sources for perceiving the will of God are the Holy Scripture, the life of Jesus Christ, the active presence of the Holy Spirit, and the fellowship and teaching of the Christian community or the church. It is therefore within this framework of faith commitment that I attempt to develop a pattern of personal morality and a guide for ethical responsibility toward all the others of my life. I do not belong to myself, but to God, and I am responsible and committed to devote myself "wholly to God and His work." Of course, I recognize that such a faith expression, as stated above, flies in the face of the "cult" of self-worship and a psychology based on the centrality of self as the key to life fulfillment. It also flies in the face of any theology that does not take seriously the fall of man, or the fact of sin and selfishness as inherent in humanity. Such a faith takes the Incarnation historically and knows nothing of the "myth of Christ" or of the "Christ of myth." Such a faith looks to the God who has become Emmanuel in Jesus Christ and to the real presence of that God in the Holy Spirit as promised by Jesus Christ. With this kind of God it is possible to aspire to holiness of heart and life. It seems to me that both the personal and social aspects of moral and ethical behavior are explicit in the words of John Wesley. If the church is to be liberated for witness and ministry, we must again aspire to seek such a life—in all of life.

It is certainly beyond the scope or intention of this book to deal with all the myriad questions in the realm of private or public morality and ethical responsibility. I have chosen to deal with five basic issues which are currently debated hotly in and outside the church. There are others which, in your mind, may be just as, or more, important. I do not wish to argue that point. It will be my intention to look at the issues to be discussed within the framework of what it means to practice holiness of heart and life.

First, I choose to discuss the realm of human sexuality, the current sexual revolution in society which is challenging the traditional Christian teaching of monogamous marriage as the God-given order for sexual relationships. I see two basic arenas where Christians are called today to make a moral decision in the face of conflicting social practices. The first is cohabitation outside marriage with persons of the opposite sex. Here I would include the growing attitude that it is all right for any two consenting adult persons of the opposite sex to have sex together. The second issue is the whole question of homosexuality. What does the Christian faith have to say about the reality of homosexual orientation and about homosexual practice?

One other related moral dilemma of our time is the question of abortion, which may be one of the most critical moral questions Christians are called to face today. Next, I propose to look at the question of racial inclusiveness as a primary teaching of the Christian faith and the practice of racism as one of the tragic sins and problems of our times. Finally, I will deal with the problem of the poor and dispossessed. What is the Christian's responsibility to the poor, and what does this say about the life-style of the Christian in affluent America? It seems to me that each of these questions has to do with both personal faith and moral practice and with social responsibility and the making of ethical choice in the social community. What does it mean to have and to practice holiness of heart and life, as we make our choices and live out our lives as disciples of Jesus Christ?

On Human Sexuality

First, let us look at the whole question of human sexuality. In the first chapter of the Scriptures we read "And God created man in His own image, in the image of God He created him; male and female He created them. And God blessed them; and God said to them, 'Be fruitful and multiply and fill the earth'" (Gen. 1:27-28a). Man and woman are recognized as sexual creatures by creation and by the natural order of things. We read further and find that "God saw all that He had made, and behold, it was very good" (Gen. 1:31a). From the beginning God put His stamp of approval on the sexual nature of human beings as a good part of His creation. Whether we read these verses allegorically or historically, it would appear that the Judeo-Christian tradition, from its inception, has seen sexuality in terms of male-female relationships and as good.

Sexuality is not to be viewed only in terms of an action, of intercourse to be entered into between man and woman for procreational or fulfillment purposes in a physical sense; it is also to be understood in a spiritual and psychological sense where male and female complement each other in the created order of things. Certainly it is possible for individual men and women to lead a good life apart from a strictly sexual (physical) relationship with a member of the opposite sex. At the same time, many of us from within the framework of marriage and the family want to witness to the truth of our own experience that we have found a more ultimate humanity in the fulfillment of our lives in a close personal relationship—physical as well as spiritual and psychological—with a member of the opposite sex. We see ourselves as being more than we could have ever become without this relationship.

Our attitude toward the physical consummation of our sexuality may well be governed by our presuppositions about the nature of human beings. Do we live in a deterministic world, where evolution by chance and the survival of the fittest explain our origin? Or, do we live in a created universe where we are made in the image of God—with a mind, will, and spirit uniquely different from the rest of creation—and where we have come to our present state of being, however that has happened, within a divinely ordered universe? For some of us at least, in this last third of the twentieth century, the latter is more logical and intellectually compatible with our experience and the knowledge presently available to humanity.

My presuppositions are that we are part of a created order of things which includes male and female as spiritual beings made in the image of God. Scripture and the tradition of which I am a part tell me that procreation is a basic reason for my sexuality. Reason and personal experience also confirm this in my life. In addition the fulfillment of my basic humanity as referred to above, in a sense not known apart from the male-female relationship, is also a part of my experience. Such an understanding of the natural order of things, including our sexuality, that is creational in concept, makes more sense to me than a closed deterministic universe. Therefore, if I am to be logical and true in my witness and affirmation concerning human sexuality, I must affirm that we are sexual because we are male-female, and that a legitimate or divinely approved sexual relationship is male-female, and *that it is good.*

Further, I maintain that the intended place for sexual consummation and fulfillment is within the bounds of marriage and the family. Many people today who thought that they would play at sex or marriage by a liaison of convenience or pleasure have found that their lives were shattered when they put too cheap a value on their sexuality. If we are male and female, made in the image of God, then our relationships must have value beyond instinct and fulfillment of physical pleasure. If this is not true, then we are no more than animals. As I have studied the Scriptures for these twenty-five years in the ministry, and as I have prayed about my role as prophet, pastor, and priest, I have been increasingly convinced that we, male and female, are meant to relate to each other in sexual intimacy in monogamous marriage for life. Marriage is a covenant wherein the man is to love his wife, "as Christ also loved the church and gave Himself up for her." As the husband gives his life up for his wife and is subject to her, so also should wives give their lives up to their husbands and be subject to them (Eph. 5:21-31). In the marriage relationship, the participants must relate in an attitude of interdependence far more than independence. In the self-assertive and self-affirming psychological climate of today this may sound old hat, but as Professor Vitz points out, "a high degree of assertive autonomy is impossible in any serious long-term relationship."[3] We still gain life, even in marriage, by giving and losing ourselves in covenant commitment to each other.

Marriage, and therefore the family, on a life-commitment basis, is also the most logical and likely place where children can love and obey their parents and where parents can most responsibly meet the needs of their children. Though there is much failure in the modern family and home, it is not because of the nature of the institution as such, but, because humanity—male and female—is not willing to live out the covenant as God intended.

What About Homosexuality?

What does this say about homosexuality? It is the clear teaching of both the Old and the New Testaments that the practice of homosexuality is forbidden in the Judeo-Christian tradition. This teaching is plainly embedded in the teaching of Israel. In the story of the destruction of Sodom (Gen. 19:1-26), the practice of homosexuality is held up to be an abomination so great as to merit destruction. Of course, there were other sins in Sodom such as idolatry, injustice, and unrighteousness, but sodomy or homosexuality is pictured as being the essence of the sin of Sodom. Likewise in Leviticus, homosexual practice is clearly condemned. "You shall not lie with male as one lies with a female; it is an abomination." . . . "If there is a man who lies with a male as those who lie with a woman, both of them have committed a detestable act" (Lev. 18:22; 20:13).

One of the clearest teachings against homosexual practice is to be found in Romans. Paul speaks plainly about homosexuality as a sin that naturally follows when the creature or humanity is put at the center of things, and God is not obeyed and worshiped as God.

For the wrath of God is revealed from heaven against all ungodliness and unrighteousness of men, who suppress the truth in unrighteousness, because that which is known about God is evident within them; for God made it evident to them. For since the creation of the world His invisible attributes, His eternal power and divine nature, have been clearly seen, being understood through what has been made, so that they are without excuse. For even though they knew God, they did not honor Him as God, or give thanks; but they became futile in their speculations, and their foolish heart was darkened. Professing to be wise, they became fools, and exchanged the glory of the incorruptible God for an image in the form of corruptible man and of birds and four-footed animals and crawling creatures.

Therefore God gave them over in the lusts of their hearts to impurity, that their bodies might be dishonored among them. For they exchanged the truth of God for a lie, and worshiped and served the creature rather than the Creator, who is blessed forever. Amen.

For this reason God gave them over to degrading passions; for their women exchanged the natural function for that which is unnatural, and in the same way also the men abandoned the natural function of the woman and burned in their desire toward one another, men with men committing indecent acts and receiving in their own persons the due penalty of their error.

And just as they did not see fit to acknowledge God any longer, God gave them over to a depraved mind, to do those things which are not proper (Rom. 1:18-28).

While Jesus did not specifically condemn homosexuality, He clearly affirmed marriage as the divinely directed relationship between man and woman. A man is not directed to leave his father and mother and be joined to another man, but to be joined "to his wife; and the two shall become one flesh. Consequently they are no longer two, but one flesh" (Matt. 19:5-6). Some would counter with the theology that Jesus Christ accepts us just as we are and affirms our humanity. Further it is said that this is what it means to experience salvation or liberation through Jesus Christ. There is partial truth in this position. Jesus Christ does accept us as we are when we turn to Him; but, in that acceptance, if we accept it, we find ourselves changed. He never leaves us where we are, and He does not approve of aberrations in our behavior whether they be social, racial, or sexual in nature. Surely homosexuality is an aberration of God's intended order of things, is opposed by the teaching of Scripture, and is therefore, not to be sanctioned by the Christian church.

Christ might well say to the homosexual, condemned by a judgmental and unloving church, what he said to the

woman taken in adultery: "Did no one condemn you? . . .
Neither do I condemn you." But He would quickly add, "Go
. . . and sin no more." And just as clearly as He was talking
about the woman's adultery, He would be talking about the
homosexual's relationships with persons of the same sex.

That the church has not shown the love and compassion
toward the homosexual that it should is clear to me. If we are
to be the reconciling and redeeming community that God
calls us to be, we must seek the guidance of the Holy Spirit so
we can relate with love and healing toward the homosexual.
This does not mean that we must accept or approve of
homosexual behavior, any more than God approves of some
of our sinful acts or thoughts, while at the same time loving
us redemptively. But, as ones who have been forgiven, and
continue to be forgiven, for our sins and who are reconciled
to God through His gracious and mighty act of redemption in
Jesus Christ, we must reach out with love and reconciliation
to the homosexual person. This we have not done. In our
judgmental and unloving attitude toward the homosexual,
we are guilty of sin against God and against our neighbor.
Before we can be redemptive in our relationship with the
homosexual, we so-called "straight" Christians must seek
God's forgiveness for our own sins of fear, lack of love, and
harsh judgment. It will not always be easy or pleasant as we
seek to affirm the person without giving approval to the
practice. In fact, this is most difficult to do in a truly
reconciling and redemptive way; but, God calls us to walk in
the Spirit and pattern of Jesus Christ as reconciling agents for
Him in and to the world. Holiness of heart and life certainly
involves a loving witness and attitude, even toward those
with whom we strongly disagree.

Is Abortion Holy?

What does holiness of heart and life have to say about the
question of abortion? Probably no other moral or ethical

question is debated more seriously and stridently in America today than that of abortion. Since the 1973 Supreme Court decision, the law of the land has practically allowed so-called "abortion on demand" as the natural or basic right of any woman. In effect, if a woman becomes pregnant and determines that the birth of the child she has conceived will work economic or social hardship on her or her family; if it is thought that the child might be defective physically or mentally; if the unwanted pregnancy threatens the psychological, mental, or physical health of the mother; or if the mother-to-be just does not want the child, then she can determine on her own and without her husband's or the child's father's consent to have a legal abortion. This right of abortion is essentially absolute and within the discretion of the mother-to-be within the first three months of pregnancy. From a practical viewpoint, however, the result has been that anyone who wants to have an abortion can probably obtain one legally up to and through the first six months of pregnancy.

Yes, abortion is legal; but, is it morally right and ethically responsible in the light of the teaching of the Scripture and the providence of God for our lives? Do women—or men—have the right to do with their bodies as they will? Further, is the so-called "fetus" a natural extension of the mother's body, or is it a living being in the womb of a woman from the moment of conception? Obviously, from a genetic standpoint that which is conceived is potentially complete toward humanness from the point of conception. As a matter of interest, what is being aborted during the various stages of pregnancy? The heartbeat of the unborn child begins at about three weeks and brain waves can be recorded at forty days. Recorded brain waves are one of the recognized signs of life in a seriously injured person, and are often the determining factor in continuing or ceasing life-support systems for the critically injured. By eleven or twelve weeks the unborn child breathes liquid, has fingernails and eyelashes, and begins to suck his or her thumb. By seventeen weeks or just four months, the vocal cords begin to work and the baby can cry. The little human-to-be has all the intended parts of anatomy in place and is just waiting to be born at the proper time. What does it mean to remove such a reality from the womb of a mother and destroy it?

The Christian faith and the Christian church have been unambiguous in saying no to abortion until very recent times. Scripture references signifying that God Himself is involved in the life-giving process are numerous indeed. I will list as illustrative only a few. From the very beginning of the biblical account it is clear that the divine intention is for children to be born through sexual union of man and woman "And God created man in His own image, in the image of God He created him; male and female He created them. And God blessed them; and God said to them, 'Be fruitful and multiply, and fill the earth, and subdue it'" (Gen. 1:27-28a). When Jacob met Esau after they had been parted several years, Jacob had his wives and children with him. Esau saw the women and children and asked: "Who are these with you?" So he said, "The children whom God has graciously given your servant" (Gen. 33:5). In Psalms we read:

Behold, children are a gift of the Lord:
The fruit of the womb is a reward.   (Ps. 127:3)

In the prophecy of Isaiah to Israel, the prophet clearly depicts God as being involved in the giving of life.

Thus says the Lord, your Redeemer,
and the one who formed you from the womb.   (Isa. 44:24)

More explicitly it is stated in Psalm 139:

For Thou didst form my inward parts;
Thou didst weave me in my mother's womb.

73

I will give thanks to Thee, for I am fearfully
  and wonderfully made;
Wonderful are Thy works,
And my soul knows it very well.
My frame was not hidden from Thee,
When I was made in secret,
And skillfully wrought in the depths of the earth.
Thine eyes have seen my unformed substance;
And in Thy book they were all written,
The days that were ordained for me,
When as yet there was not one of them.   (Ps. 139:13-16)

Within the New Testament the records of the birth of Jesus
and of John the Baptist clearly depict the reality of life, yes
even sacred life—before physical birth. "Now the birth of
Jesus Christ was as follows. When His mother Mary had been
betrothed to Joseph, before they came together she was
found to be with child by the Holy Spirit" (Matt. 1:18).

After Mary had been informed by an angel about the birth
of Jesus, she went immediately to her cousin Elizabeth who
had miraculously conceived in her old age. Mary greeted
Elizabeth:

And it came about that when Elizabeth heard Mary's greeting, the
baby leaped in her womb; and Elizabeth was filled with the Holy
Spirit. And she cried out with a loud voice, and said, "Blessed
among women are you, and blessed is the fruit of your womb! And
how has it happened to me, that the mother of my Lord should come
to me? For behold, when the sound of your greeting reached my
ears, the baby leaped in my womb for joy" (Luke 1:41-44).

At that time Mary was just beginning her pregnancy and
Elizabeth was in her sixth month. One can hardly imagine
any talk here about the unborn infants carried by Mary or
Elizabeth not being life, precious life indeed, though unborn
at that time.

The Judeo-Christian tradition has always placed a deep

significance on reverence for life and for the family. Some of us are convinced that the abortion of approximately nine million unborn children in this country since 1973 is a betrayal of that tradition of reverence for life. Some have even called it the "Abortion Holocaust." I am convinced that it is wrong and against the will of God!

In a chapter on "Selfism and the Family," Paul Vitz contrasts the Christian and the selfist approach.

In contrast to selfist psychology, traditional Christianity and Judaism actively support the family and the community. For the Christian the family is the basic model for society. Father, mother, brother, and sister are common terms for Christians in both Catholic and Protestant communities. All Christians are brothers and sisters as members in the mystical body of Christ represented on earth by the mother church. Everywhere the social emphasis of the church is on integration and synthesis. Judaism's remarkably strong support for the family is also well known. Many have explained Jewish survival in terms of this reverence for family.

For Christianity, the family is a small-scale living embodiment of much of its theology: God the Father, Christ the Son, Mary the Mother, all of us as children of God are prominent biblical themes. May we not then view an ideology which systematically denigrates or attacks the family, by structural analogy, as a force attacking Christianity? Consider, too, the central holy day of Christmas, which is a joyous celebration of motherhood and birth. May we not see that a psychologist advising abortion is acting in hostility against the deep structure of beliefs and meaning celebrated in the Christmas story? Recall that the young Mary was pregnant under circumstances that today routinely terminate in abortion. In the important theological context of Christmas the killing of an unborn child is a symbolic killing of the Christ child.[4]

Some may think this is too hard and harsh. I do not think so. Ultimately, what "abortion on demand" signifies is the lessening of reverence for all of life. It is but a short step from a permissive and affirming attitude toward abortion—the taking of an unborn life—to the elimination of the handicapped or retarded, and to euthanasia—the killing of the senile and "unproductive" aged. In all of our rightful concern today about human rights, especially of the poor and oppressed, who is to speak for the defenseless unborn child? Does not this one who has been conceived in the mother's womb have any right to life? The abortion tragedy has not so much to do with rights as with responsibility to live before God as His children with reverence for all life.

But you may ask, "What about the personal rights of a woman—or a man—over her or his own body?" Again, let me affirm that the disciple is one who has made a life commitment to Jesus Christ as Savior and Lord, and does not keep or exercise control over his or her life, apart from God's will. We do not own ourselves, even our own bodies. We belong to God!

Then others say that to forbid abortion is a kind of absolutism that is no longer acceptable to modern humanity. To which I would rejoin, "Is the only absolute left the illogical philosophy of relativism that 'there are no absolutes'?" Surely such a position about truth and ethics, though widely held, can be clearly seen by thinking persons as nonsense. Is it less of an absolute to say that abortion is right or good (one could hardly argue for doing that which is not right or good) than it is to say that abortion is wrong? Can any of us or all of us do what we please for our comfort and pleasure irrespective of the teaching of God? Is it possible that when we have put our "selves" and our "rights" at the center of life, without listening to the word of God and being submissive to God Himself, that we have set our paths toward destruction? It is my conviction that we have! And, regardless of what the state says, or continues to say about abortion, it is clear to me that the Christian must say no! Life begins at conception, and only where the mother's life is clearly endangered should abortion ever be considered. I recognize that there are perplexing and very difficult life situations with which we are confronted. All of us have great concern about such things as incest and rape, or the burden of unwanted pregnancies—particularly in the face of poverty. I do not want to judge harshly anyone who faces the difficulties of life—sometimes tragic life. Suffice it to say if we are to have and live holiness of heart and life, we need a far greater reverence for life and acceptance of responsibility for our actions than is evidenced in the abortion tragedy of our time. Surely our culture, and our church insofar as we have given approval to the aborting of the unborn, come under the judgment of God. We in the church, if we are to be true to the biblical faith and the Judeo-Christian tradition out of which we come, must again speak with a clear voice on this issue. We must affirm that while abortions may have the legal sanction of government, in the eyes and teaching of God and His church abortion is morally and spiritually wrong.

VI

Holiness of Heart and Life (II)

For you are all sons of God through faith in Christ Jesus. For all of you who were baptized into Christ have clothed yourselves with Christ. There is neither Jew nor Greek, there is neither slave nor free man, there is neither male nor female; for you are all one in Christ Jesus. And if you belong to Christ, then you are Abraham's offspring, heirs according to promise.

(Gal. 3:26-29)

The Inclusive Church

It has often been said that the most segregated hour of the week is eleven o'clock on Sunday morning. Perhaps that is true, but, if it is, it is only symbolic of a schism in relationship that exists in society between race and class. Certainly, the disciple of Jesus Christ who reads the Scriptures and is open to its clear teaching has no room for social prejudice in his heart or life. The one who lives a life of holiness knows the God-given mandate, within the family of faith, that we are all one in Jesus Christ. Nowhere is this more plainly stated than in Paul's letter to the Galatian church as quoted above.

In the second chapter of Ephesians, Paul writes to the Gentiles about their now being included, through faith in Jesus Christ, in the covenant family of God.

Therefore remember, that formerly you, the Gentiles in the flesh, who are called "Uncircumcision" by the so-called "Circumcision," which is performed in the flesh by human hands—remember that you were at that time separate from Christ, excluded from the commonwealth of Israel, and strangers to the covenants of promise, having no hope and without God in the world. But now in Christ Jesus you who formerly were far off have been brought near by the blood of Christ. For He Himself is our peace, who made both groups into one, and broke down the barrier of the dividing wall, by abolishing in His flesh the enmity, which is the Law of commandments contained in ordinances, that in Himself He might make the two into one new man, thus establishing peace, and might reconcile them both in one body to God through the cross, by having put to death the enmity. AND HE CAME AND PREACHED PEACE TO YOU WHO WERE FAR AWAY, AND PEACE TO THOSE WHO WERE NEAR; for through Him we both have our access in one Spirit to the Father. (Eph. 2:11-18)

For both the Jew and the Gentile of that day, these were impossible words to accept in the face of the history and teaching of Israel, and according to all the traditions of society. The Jew and the Gentile could not be one; but, the little Pharisee from Tarsus—a Jew of the Jews—was stating that this is what the coming of Jesus Christ meant for humanity. Walls were to be broken down and people were to be brought together in Jesus Christ. Peace for our hearts and peace among all of us are God-given gifts of faith in Jesus Christ. While that is the biblical teaching, the practice in society, and in the church, does not reflect the biblical teaching. Surely then, the church of Jesus Christ must speak prophetically and act redemptively in the face of overt or covert racism.

I am not at all sure that the white church, which I know best, is ready to do that. Nor, am I sure that the ethnic church is ready either, especially many of the leaders of the ethnic church. Not only are there valid differences in tradition and culture on both sides, which are hard to overcome, but also there are attitudes of hatred and prejudice on both sides, which are hard to overcome. And if any member of any ethnic church reacts too strongly to what I am saying, may I suggest that you examine your own heart to ascertain whether you are really willing to accept this WASP as your brother. Commitment to an inclusive church must become our commitment to God, and to one another, if we are to find liberation for witness and ministry. We must truly do all within our will and faith to become brothers and sisters in Jesus Christ. That is, we must be willing to deal not only with the racism and prejudice of the white race, but also with the racism of ethnic pride or ethnic chauvinism. Just as it is wrong, very wrong, for an Anglo-Saxon to have a false and bigoted pride, because of race or heritage, toward other races, so it is also wrong, very wrong, for any of the brown, red, yellow, or black races to speak or think of their race as superior or better than others. We are all part of a fallen race, the human race, and our only hope is in the new race which was begun in Jesus Christ.

Professor Orlando Patterson of Howard University sees a hidden danger in the ethnic revival.

Ethnic pluralism, however dressed up in liberal rhetoric, has no place whatever in a democratic society based on the humanistic ideals of our Judeo-Christian ethic. It is, first, socially divisive. However much the more liberal advocates may claim the contrary, the fact remains that the glorification of one's heritage and one's group always implies its "chosen-ness" over all others. . . . Ethnicity emphasizes the trivialities that distinguish us and obscures the overwhelming reality of our common genetic and human heritages as well as our common needs and hopes. By emphasizing differences, ethnicity lends itself to the conservative belief in the inevitability of inequality. It is no accident that the neo-conservative thinkers have all hailed the revival.[1]

One of the places where ethnic chauvinism is most evident is in the imposition of disproportionate quotas on our national boards and agencies. The *Discipline* of the church now recommends that at least 25 percent of the membership of general boards and agencies be racial and ethnic minority persons. There are at least two reasons why this will ultimately be counterproductive. First, it is not basically democratic in principle and provides approximately 500 percent more per-capita representation than from the rest of the church. I know many of the respected leaders of the church who privately believe this is wrong, but who will not speak out because they fear being branded racist or reactionary. Inevitably, this kind of psychologically and/or legally enforced quota system of overrepresentation will create further and more deep-seated resentment. It will not bring healing and reconciliation, but will in the end increase racism. Though perhaps I may be branded as racist for speaking so plainly, I know my own heart and believe strongly that what I am saying must be said in the long-range interest of a truly inclusive church.

The requirement that the professional staff of the general boards and agencies be at least 25 percent ethnic minority, and in the case of the Board of Church and Society, 33 percent ethnic minority, is invalid for the same reasons indicated above. Perhaps it would be justifiable to allow for overrepresentation up to, say, twice the number of ethnic representatives as there would be proportionally, but to go to the extent which has been done is neither democratic nor wise. But the ethnics, joined by the youth and feminist caucuses, and the secular renewalists have intimidated much of the leadership of the church who are either afraid of the charge of racism or are expunging a sense of guilt for past sins of the church. For several years now, and continuing through at least 1984, the church has been asked to give special support to the Ethnic Minority Local Church Apportionment Fund Program. I believe in this emphasis, and the church of which I am pastor has faithfully fulfilled its responsibilities in this area. But the quota system is helping to undermine the ethnic minority local church. Many of the more capable ordained ethnic pastors of the church have chosen to accept the lure of a staff assignment with the title and prestige of a national board position. With the percentage being allocated to the ethnic part of the church being several times a proportional representation, there has been a leadership drain on the local church. If those who are in such positions are truly interested in the local church, I challenge them to voluntarily return to the pastorate where, and only where, the church can be built.

To a large extent it is true that there is not an "open itinerancy" for ethnics in the church at large. But, this is a problem which cuts both ways. I know of few white pastors who have the will or the ability to sensitively and culturally identify and minister to an ethnic congregation. In fact, when I volunteered to consider such an appointment for myself while serving on the cabinet of a liberal bishop, I was told that it wouldn't wash and that it was out of the question. I agree that it might not have worked; but unless some of us are willing to lose our lives in risk and servant-ministry, instead of seeking title and position, how shall we prove the teaching of Jesus Christ about servanthood in our day? Remember that it was said about Jesus Christ,

Have this attitude in yourselves which was also in Christ Jesus, who, although He existed in the form of God, did not regard equality with God a thing to be grasped, but emptied Himself, taking the form of a bond-servant, and being made in the likeness of men. And being found in appearance as a man, He humbled Himself by becoming obedient to the point of death, even death on a cross. (Phil. 2:5-8)

In response to the request of the mother of the sons of Zebedee who asked for special privilege for each of them, Jesus replied to all of the disciples: "Whoever wishes to become great among you shall be your servant . . . just as the Son of Man did not come to be served, but to serve, and to give His life as a ransom for many" (Matt. 20:26, 28).

I have served on a general board staff as the general secretary and as an associate-general secretary. I voluntarily left such a position to go back to the local pastorate because I was not willing to lose my own soul in the brokerage of power and privilege in the hierarchy of the church. Special interest and pressure groups in the church are a significant part of this quest for the right to exercise power. One of these days perhaps each group which is fighting for its "rights" may feel it has succeeded; but, I suspect that in such an arena the Savior of the world will be forgotten and will have long since departed such a distorted picture of the body of Christ. I love my church too much not to risk being prophetic in the face of such a prospect.

Within the church community, there must be an inclusive fellowship if it is to be the body of Christ. However, it is certainly fitting and right that such a fellowship include the continuance of primarily ethnic churches either because of language, cultural traditions, or neighborhood. These churches deserve the support of the whole church so long as each part recognizes others, and is recognized by others, as an authentic part of the body of Christ. It is going to take a lot of praying and loving, a lot of listening and learning, and above all a deep commitment to the servanthood of Jesus Christ in each of us to break down the walls so that we can truly become one body in Christ. I for one hope that the inclusive church will keep some of the diversity in styles of worship, as expressed in the ethnic church, so that the richness of the church will not be lessened. My own life has been immeasurably enriched through worshiping with black congregations.

I do not know very well the Hispanic, the native American, or the Asian-American church. I know more, though not nearly enough, about the black church. Ethnic members in the church where I now serve are active in membership and leadership. During the more than five years that I was a district superintendent, I was the lone white member of the Black Community Development Council related to The United Methodist Church in Fort Worth, Texas. During that time, we reopened a vacant church in a neighborhood which had radically changed in racial composition. Frankly, it was difficult to get the pastors of the neighboring churches to cooperate in recruiting laypersons to begin ministry to a community where we had no viable ministry. Perhaps racism was part of the problem, but I suspect that just plain old unenlightened and parochial selfishness was the principle failure in leadership.

My wife, Sally, was one of the first volunteers to help begin a study group and a day care center, and for over four years she belonged to the "pepper and salt" covenant group which became the Eastwood United Methodist Church. During this time she served with and under the leadership of two black pastors.

We are committed to the inclusive church, and I will continue to speak and act prophetically in my own life for racial inclusiveness and for equal opportunity for all in and through the church of Jesus Christ. This is my commitment; it is the reason why I am willing to risk saying what I have said here.

In January of 1972, I concluded an article about the necessity of becoming an inclusive church with this paragraph.

It is my conviction, as a disciple of Jesus Christ, that we will find peace, love, and brotherhood together, or not at all. I am not sure that any of us are working at this hard enough, but I am sure that most of the white majority have not come to terms with the question at all. Time is short for us to act. We must move toward creating a truly inclusive church. In one man's opinion we shall find the answer together or not at all.

Today I would add one thought to the above paragraph. I am not sure that any of us, ethnic or otherwise, have the proper servant-commitment to truly build an inclusive church which is liberated for witness and ministry. I still believe that time is short—and certainly much less than when I wrote the article eight years ago.

How Then Shall I Live?

For we have brought nothing into the world, so we cannot take anything out of it either. And if we have food and covering, with these we shall be content. But those who want to get rich fall into temptation and a snare and many foolish and harmful desires which plunge men into ruin and destruction. For the love of money is the root of all sorts of evil, and some by longing for it have wandered away from the faith, and pierced themselves with many a pang.
(I Tim. 6:7-10)

What does holiness of heart and life have to do with the life-style of a disciple of Jesus Christ? In a further exhortation to Timothy, Paul writes about the difficult times of the last days when "men will be lovers of self, lovers of money, . . . lovers of pleasure rather than lovers of God" (II Tim. 3:2-4). It has been relatively easy for Christians to agree with the condemnation of sexual sins such as adultery and homosexuality as recorded in Scripture. It has not been so easy, though, to accept the fact that the same Scripture lists greed and self-centered pleasure-seeking as sins equally condemned by God. It should not be that difficult, however, for any of us to understand that when we put self and our own desires at the center of our lives, the result will inevitably be sin, in both a personal and social sense. It is my deep conviction that the affluence and ease-centered mode of most of our lives in the established church today is one of the greatest barriers to liberation for witness and ministry. We are so busy taking care of our "wants," not just our "needs," that we do not have the time or even the inclination to be more than casually concerned about other people and their needs. Least of all do we evidence our concern for the poor and the oppressed. And yet, if we are biblical Christians we should remember the first message given by Jesus in the synagogue at Nazareth.

And the book of the prophet Isaiah was handed to Him. And He opened the book, and found the place where it was written,

"THE SPIRIT OF THE LORD IS UPON ME,

BECAUSE HE ANOINTED ME TO PREACH THE GOSPEL TO THE POOR.

HE HAS SENT ME TO PROCLAIM RELEASE TO THE CAPTIVES,

AND RECOVERY OF SIGHT TO THE BLIND,

TO SET FREE THOSE WHO ARE DOWNTRODDEN,

TO PROCLAIM THE FAVORABLE YEAR OF THE LORD."

And He closed the book and gave it back to the attendant, and sat down; and the eyes of all in the synagogue were fixed upon Him. And He began to say to them, "Today this Scripture has been fulfilled in your hearing." (Luke 4:17-21)

In the early days of Methodism this pattern of Jesus in preaching to the poor and the oppressed was observed literally by John Wesley and his followers. They preached to the poor and oppressed miners in the fields outside their mine shafts. They visited the prisoners in jail. They went to people outside the church, wherever they could be found and told them of the judgment of God on the sin in their lives, and of the wonderful grace of God which was available to bring forgiveness and pardon to their lives. They spoke of a God who had come close to them in Jesus Christ and who was interested in all their lives. Further, and this was unusual "Good News" in those days, they could experience and know this God through the Holy Spirit. In addition, Wesley challenged his followers to take care of widows and orphans and not to spend any money on themselves beyond that which was absolutely essential for food, clothing, and shelter. In his later years he was concerned that the people called Methodists were becoming affluent. "The Methodists grow more and more self-indulgent, because they grow rich. And it is an observation which admits of few exceptions, that nine in ten of these decreased in grace in the same proportion as they increased in wealth."[2]

In his sermon on "The Use of Money"[3] Wesley expounded on what he called his "three plain rules." *Gain all you can*—though not at the expense of your physical or mental health, nor at the hurt of anyone else. *Save all you can*—do not indulge yourself or your children beyond the plain necessities of life. *Give all you can*—since all that you are and possess belongs to God and you are but stewards for Him, use the whole of your life and possessions in witness and ministry for God. Wesley practiced what he preached in his own personal life-style and the use of his resources.

His challenge that, if he left more than 10£ in his will, anyone could call him a thief and a liar was redeemed; apart from his book concern, he left only loose money in his clothes and bureau, and 6£ for the poor man who should carry his body to the grave. During the latter part of his lfe he gave away from the profits of his books about 1,000£ a year; and is computed to have bestowed in charity not less than 30,000£ during his life-time.[4]

How does this stack up with the life-style and the use of resources of the people called Methodists today, or of any so-called mainline Christians?

I am afraid that we have become too rich and concerned about ourselves to be generous givers even of our surplus money, much less to look on our rightful Christian commitment as the careful stewardship of all of life. It is my privilege to pastor a significant downtown church, The First United Methodist Church in Peoria, Illinois. The people of this congregation are our friends and our family; they have shown us much love and care in the more than eight years I have served as their pastor. Many of them have a growing love for Jesus Christ and for one another. But as a people of God we have only begun to be faithful stewards of all the riches of the world to which God has entrusted us. The number one sin of these people, whom I love and cherish greatly, is that which afflicts much of America and the West, and most of the people called Methodists. That most crippling sin is the sin of affluence, the love of economic and social security that goes way beyond the point of need, in the face of all the need and hurt in the world. The clear teaching of the Scripture and of Jesus Christ is that Christian disciples, if they are truly His disciples, be in ministry to those in need in the world.

"But when the Son of Man comes in His glory, and all the angels with Him, then He will sit on His glorious throne. And all the nations will be gathered before Him; and He will separate them from one another, as the shepherd separates the sheep from the goats; and He will put the sheep on His right, and the goats on the left. Then the King will say to those on His right, 'Come, you who are blessed of My Father, inherit the kingdom prepared for you from the foundation of the world. For I was hungry, and you gave Me something to eat; I was thirsty, and you gave Me drink; I was a stranger, and you invited Me in; naked, and you clothed Me; I was sick, and you visited Me; I was in prison, and you came to Me.' Then the righteous will answer Him, saying, 'Lord, when did we see You hungry, and feed You, or thirsty, and give You drink? And when did we see You a stranger, and invite You in, or naked, and clothe You? And when did we see You sick, or in prison, and come to You?' And the King will answer and say to them, 'Truly I say to you, to the extent that you did it to one of these brothers of Mine, even the least of them, you did it to Me.' Then He will also say to those on His left, 'Depart from Me, accursed ones, into the eternal fire which has been prepared for the devil and his angels; for I was hungry, and you gave Me nothing to eat; I was thirsty, and you gave Me nothing to drink; I was a stranger, and you did not invite Me in; naked, and you did not clothe Me; sick, and in prison, and you did not visit Me.' Then they themselves also will answer, saying, 'Lord, when did we see You hungry, or thirsty, or a stranger, or naked, or sick, or in prison, and did not take care of You?' Then He will answer them, saying, 'Truly I say to you, to the extent that you did not do it to one of the least of these, you did not do it to Me.' And these will go away into eternal punishment, but the righteous into eternal life.'' (Matt. 25:31-46)

And yet, in the face of this clear teaching of Jesus Christ, most Christians give little of their financial resources for the ministry of Christ and His church, and even less of their time and talents in witness and ministry. The only people in our congregation, including my wife and myself, who are truly sacrificing, are a few of our senior citizens who are giving at least a tithe of their income while attempting to live on fixed retirement in a time of inflation.

This practice of affluent life, making all we can and using all we make for our own needs and pleasures, is hardly recognized as a sin at all among most churchgoers. And, this sin will be most difficult to break, because it is so deep-rooted in our tradition, culture, and our very hearts. Yes, our hearts have been sold to success as the world measures success, and we worship at the feet of the God of mammon and the idol of self. These idols must be broken and our lives turned around, it we are to be liberated for witness and ministry.

Of course, this is easier said than done—to break the hold of culture on our lives and to begin to live as radical disciples of Jesus Christ. It is almost impossible to do this alone, or even as one family; the culture and peer pressure is too great. As in other aspects of the Christian life, we need one another, and must support one another, if we are to live as radical Christians in the secular and affluent society of the West. A number of models are being tried out today, with various degrees of success. I will list and discuss briefly three of these.

The Church of the Redeemer in Houston, Texas. Charismatic renewal has occurred in this Episcopal congregation, and many members of the congregation are now living in voluntary communal arrangements of eight to fifteen members. The style of life is simple but the freedom and security of those so committed is great indeed in the face of all the perils of modern society. More importantly, the freeing-up of much time and talent for Christian witness and ministry is great indeed.

The Church of The Saviour in Washington, D.C. In this church membership is taken seriously, with four regular disciplines required of all who become members of the congregation. Each person must attend church each week, become a part of a study and prayer fellowship, be a member of a mission group, and practice proportionate giving beginning with a tithe of total gross income. The study and prayer discipline must be practiced daily as a personal discipline, and strengthened by a regular group experience at least once a week. The mission groups are varied according to the real needs and opportunities available in the community in which the church exists.

The Gospel Temple in Philadelphia, Pennsylvania. This Pentecostal church has purposefully changed the structure and style of its congregational life by dropping all existing activities but the Sunday morning worship service. The people are intentionally encouraged to come together in "home meetings" or "house churches"—Wesley would have called them "class meetings"—for study, prayer, worship, and guidance. These local or neighborhood groups became, after much trial and error, the focal center of spiritual growth and nurture in the church. Mutual support, including economic assistance for those facing financial need, has resulted from and helped create the real *koinonia* of a Christian fellowship. The church is beginning to develop and evidence real concern and involvement in reaching out beyond their own to others.

I have personally been familiar with The Church of The Saviour and the Church of the Redeemer for a number of years. These two, along with The Gospel Temple, are listed by Ronald Sider as representative attempts by some Christian groups to restructure their personal and corporate lives as professing disciples of Jesus Christ. (See Mr. Sider's book, *Rich Christians in an Age of Hunger*, paper, Paulist Press, 1977.) The Christians in these three congregations and in a number of others are attempting to find new and more radical ways to live for Jesus Christ and are taking seriously the fact that faith in Christ touches all of life. The emphasis on personal commitment and growth through study, prayer, and vital worship is common to each of these unusual congregations. In addition, the community of faith in each takes seriously the mutual responsibility of the members for one another. In two of the three a significant emphasis is on a more simple life-style and the imperative for Christians to be involved in meeting the needs of others. None of the three is a perfect model, and I do not point to them as such. It is most encouraging to me, however, to see serious and purposeful attempts being made by groups of Christians to live more effectively and faithfully as disciples of Jesus Christ. Also, I am firmly convinced that the modern church must be freed from traditional models and structures if it is to be liberated for witness and ministry.

Where does a person—where does a church congregation—where does a denomination—start to face all the hunger and need in the world, and especially in the light of our affluence? My wife and I have started with the graduated tithe. Since we became Christians we have always tithed—and that has been a tithe on our gross income before taxes. More recently, since our children are grown and away from home and we have received a larger salary, we have increased that tithe by a percentage point or two each year. This last year we gave something over 20 percent of our income to the church and in support of various mission needs at home and around the world. This has certainly not hurt us, and we cannot say that we are truly sacrificing greatly for Christ and His church. For us, it is just one simple way in which we can begin to indicate a more radical commitment to Jesus Christ and His church. For most Christians in the church today, a minimum beginning toward a radical commitment to Christian discipleship should begin with a tithe of their gross income. If that should happen on a large scale there would be literally billions of resources available, through the church, to feed the hungry and meet other needs in the world.

Let me hasten to add here that the giving of money, even a tithe or more, cannot fulfill the call of Christ for a disciple to give all of life to and for God and others. But it is a clear place to start and one measure of our commitment to Christ and His church. In the examples which I have used in this chapter, both personal and corporate, the living out of the Christian faith is demonstrated in the giving of self in servant ministry.

Indeed it is clear to me that if we are to have holiness of heart and life, we must live more like the One who had "nowhere to lay His head" (Matt. 8:20). I know of no way to begin doing what we find difficult to do except through the faith that He can do it in us, through the presence and power of His Spirit. Even to begin to accept this, much less practice it, is to believe the prayer of Jesus in John 17, when He prayed "that they may all be one; even as Thou, Father, art in Me, and I in Thee, that they also may be in Us; that the world may believe that Thou didst send Me" (John 17:21). Yes, God wants us to live out His life here on earth by opening our hearts and lives to His Holy Spirit, who is the only one who can give us holiness of heart and life. If we are to be liberated for witness and ministry, we will reflect this in our personal moral decisions and in our ethical responsibilities in all our relationships. For the one who lives the life of Christ, division has no place here.

VII

How Shall the Church Be Led?

A New Pelagianism seeks salvation in the correction of structures rather than in conversion to God; a new Gnosticism places all its hope in the apt phrase or the esoteric formula rather than in Jesus Christ crucified and risen.[1]

For a number of years a great many of us who have been privileged to participate in or closely observe the administrative and mission structure of The United Methodist Church have been increasingly alarmed at the trends we have seen both in the structure and leadership style. A preoccupation with structure and a diffusion of leadership have been critically negative on the witness and ministry of the church.

Anyone who has attended General Conference since 1968 can easily conclude that the number one priority facing the church is how it should be organized in structure to function as a church. In many ways the valuable time and energy of the delegates have been consumed with the role of church structure mechanics. And, this itself is illusionary, for most of the basic recommendations and decisions have come from the will and preplanning of board and agency staff. We have been so preoccupied with structure and change in structure that our people are confused, and we have wasted time, energy, and money in an endless process. In The United Methodist Church of today, many autonomous or semi-autonomous voices are speaking for and to the church, but no clear voice of leadership or authority is speaking a word for God to the church or to the world. Surely, anyone who is familiar with church polity and recent United Methodist church history must know that we are faced with a crisis in leadership and in confidence from church members.

This crisis in leadership was strikingly reflected in a poll of denominational leaders by the General Council on Ministries during 1979. Reporting on the poll to a meeting of Annual Conference Council Directors in El Paso, Texas, in January 1980, the Reverend Alan Waltz said that

without the will to change, the UMC will be concerned primarily with "administrating its past and describing the symptoms of its present malaise." . . .

Leaders don't see much indication that the UMC is willing to make the major reallocations of resources necessary to mount significant outreach and evangelism programs or to start new congregations. . . .

Dr. Waltz told the council directors that these pessimistic expectations "need not prevail." But to counter these pervasive trends the denomination needs a "clear sense of direction, strong leadership and a sense of expectancy and hope." . . .

Of all the issues facing the UMC, Dr. Waltz said, the need for decisive and creative leadership is perhaps the most critical. He noted that it is the paradox of our times that precisely when distrust of leaders is at its highest, we most need people to lead.

"The denomination is not against leadership per se," he said, but against leadership which is "unresponsive, committed to administering the past and interested in self-aggrandizement." . . .

Also, older organizations don't tend to value innovation; they put a premium on effective managers and administrators, he said, "As I look at annual conferences, it is apparent that it is very difficult for a pastor to 'rise' on the basis of leadership ability. They are 'disciplined' by colleagues in the ministry who accuse them of ego-building, buttering up the bishop or of looking for a better appointment." . . .

"The appointment system is one of the few surviving patronage systems left in the country," Dr. Waltz said. Patronage systems are noted for their efficiency but not for creativity. Persons are rewarded by how well they play the rules of the game, he said. . . .

And, he said, the church for at least two decades, has been training its clergy to be enablers—not leaders. To enable means to enhance the group—to submerge leadership. "We are not encouraging people to lead," he said.[2]

It seems to me that Dr. Waltz has perceptively pinpointed a very critical problem for the church. Strong leadership has been criticized so persistently in the church, even to the point of branding it pathological in nature, that only those who carefully "play the rules of the game" and become adept at the "game of process" are looked on as "safe leaders." There is little chance for risk and vision in such leadership—even less for "holy boldness" for the Lord—and just as much chance, perhaps more, for manipulation and inflicting the will of one person on the group.

There is a real sense in which the art of process in controlling the structures of the church and formulating its program has made the faith of the church a subsidiary issue and the Lord a nonparticipating bystander. For someone to suggest a day of fasting and prayer to begin a national meeting would be looked on by most leaders in today's church as a waste of time and money and a return to an outdated and ineffective expression of an uninformed primitive faith. The fact is that unless we persistently and earnestly again seek the guidance and empowering Spirit of the Lord we claim to serve, we will be the custodians of a sterile and dead religion.

When I left the General Board of Discipleship as

associate-general secretary of the Division of Evangelism, Worship and Stewardship in 1974, I wrote a general letter to all the board members and professional staff. The amount of time consumed in the process games of structure and administration was alarming to me then and is more so now. Let me quote here a part of that letter which I still affirm as a necessary word of caution and concern, and to which I do not believe the leadership of the church has yet responded with appropriate action; or possibly it may not even have been heard.

What I am about to say, I believe I am saying prophetically. One of the symptoms of death or decline in any organization or structured entity in society, whether it be in the field of government, business, education, or religion is when that organization begins to spend more and more time on its own internal organization process, rather than on the primary purpose for its existence. We have arrived at a crisis time in the life of the church in this area. The grass roots of the church, and that now includes me, is tired of the church spending so much of its time on restructuring itself. If the leaders of the church, of which you are one, do not soon move away from an almost obsession over structure, you are going to lose further support of the people whose primary concern is message and mission. While I did not feel that our present structure was the best possible at the last General Conference, I implore you to try to make what you have work. The crisis in the world is too critical and the need too great for us to continue primarily as church structure mechanics. I for one do not plan to spend a great deal more of my time in meeting with professional churchmen about structure and process in the church. The essential purpose of the staff is to serve the church at the grass-roots level and not primarily to meet with each other about the church.

Please forgive me if you feel that I am too blunt or positive here, but I am convinced that both staff and board are spending far too much time on matters not central to the propagation of the gospel and the building up of the body of Christ. Surely all of us agree that the church at the local level has reacted very negatively toward programs handed down from "above." It seems to me that as we have moved away from authoritative programming, we are increasingly in danger of being ensnared and enamored with process and structure to the detriment of the mission and ministry of the church.

Lest anyone get the idea that mine is a singular voice, or that there is no wide support for the position I am taking, let me illustrate further by quoting a few very diverse voices from across the church who have expressed similar concerns.

Dr. Earl Brewer, a professor at Chandler School of Theology, addressed the Southeastern Jurisdictional Conference at Lake Junaluska, North Carolina, in July 1980. Under the byline of Sharon Mielke in the August 1, 1980, edition of the *United Methodist Reporter*, Dr. Brewer's address was reported.

United Methodism today is a "structure without spirit" which John Wesley would disown—were the church's founder to return—a church sociologist told delegates here to the Southeastern Jurisdictional Conference.

"Spirit and structure go together or they do not go at all," Dr. Earl Brewer, a professor at UM-related Chandler School of Theology, told the 564 delegates. He said that while United Methodism has become increasingly bureaucratized, there is "real question about the grasp of the spirit" on the denomination. . . .

Secular planning processes used by the church to bureaucratically set human goals are inadequate for the Christian prayerfully seeking to understand God's goals for us.[3]

In *Newscope* dated March 25, 1977, the lead article carried the synopsis title: PREDICTS REVOLT AGAINST THE GENERAL AGENCIES.

Either the national boards and agencies will help the church get moving in mission—or, "I think, there will be a revolt against you," Jameson Jones, president of Iliff School of Theology in Denver, Colo. told the denomination's General Council on Ministries

(GCOM) at the opening session of its semi-annual meeting in Dayton.

The "final test" of the general agencies of the church, of the structures of United Methodism, Jones said, is "whether or not they facilitate vital ministry, whether or not they help the church fulfill its mission."[4]

It should be obvious that Dr. Jones thought there was a valid question as to whether or not the church was properly moving in mission, and whether or not the structure was working to facilitate missions. I strongly feel that the question raised by Dr. Jones was valid in 1977, and is even more so now.

Dr. Albert Outler, distinguished professor of theology at Perkins School of Theology, Southern Methodist University, told the Council of Bishops in their spring meeting in 1979 that the church faced a "constitutional crisis." Dr. Outler told the Council:

"There are many more United Methodists who know who they are as members of the Body of Christ than who understand and trust their leaders." [According to Dr. Outler] "that has brought about a 'constitutional crisis' in which the lines of authority and responsibility are blurred.

"The spiritual and temporal interests of our entire church are not being overseen as effectually as our crisis requires," Dr. Outler said. Unless some reform is initiated by the 1980 General Conference, "even a minor prophet can promise you disaster down the way.

"Part of the crisis," said the theologian who is credited as the main architect of the church's 'Doctrinal Statement' adopted in 1972, "is that bishops are not acting scriptural *'episkopos'*" (the New Testament word meaning "overseer" and translated as "bishop"). "That does not mean the bishop is the 'big enchilada,'" Dr. Outler said, "but rather the chief pastor with a ministry of caring, deriving 'authority for oversight from the consent of the overseen.'"

"The 'huge and quasi-autonomous bureaucracy' whose executive staffs have come to dominate the legislative processes of General

Conference is another reason why the UMC has a constitutional crisis," he declared. "They constitute a 'general superintendency'—which since the time of Asbury has been understood as the sign and agency of the episcopal office in American Methodism," he said.[5]

Professor Outler further delineates the constitutional and structural crisis faced by the church in a feature article in *The Circuit Rider,* November/December 1979. Dr. Outler points out that there is a serious conflict in different sections of the *Discipline,* concerning leadership roles and responsibility in the church.

The fact is that 'the people called Methodists' are not all that well-connected any more; and, what is more, the fact that the system isn't working as well as the times demand calls our pragmatism into question.

Who Is in Charge?
  One of the causes of this creeping malaise is the generally unrecognized (or unacknowledged) fact that our current *Book of Discipline* is cross-eyed and has been since 1972. Part I, The Constitution looks toward an episcopal polity, organized around our historic conference-system. Part IV, Chapter Seven, Administrative Order reflects and looks toward a curial polity, conglomerated as a complex bureaucracy.[6]

As pointed out by Dr. Outler, the Constitution assigns a broad authority and responsibility to the Council of Bishops.

There shall be a Council of Bishops composed of all the bishops of The United Methodist Church. The council shall meet at least once a year and plan for the general oversight and promotion of the temporal and spiritual interests of the entire Church and for carrying into effect the rules, regulations, and responsibilities prescribed and enjoined by the General Conference and in accord with the provisions set forth in this plan of Union. (Paragraph 52)[7]

In practice, whatever oversight of the church that is exercised today—and there is real question whether any effective oversight is being exercised—is somewhat nebulously assigned to the General Council on Ministries. In speaking about the effectiveness of administrative order in the church, Dr. Outler states:

everything focuses on a congery of councils, committees, commissions and boards, each with its own ambitious portfolio. In no case is there a clear line of accountability that reaches beyond any given board's special constituency. Inevitably, therefore, what has developed is a sort of administrative feudal system with separate fiefdoms, each with its ambitious chieftains and loyal coteries.

Even with all the good men and women whom we have for leaders, we are simply not getting the sort of vigorous and farsighted general oversight that our polity requires for a church like ours to function at its best. Thus, I have concluded that if General Conference doesn't begin to resolve this crisis, the way beyond 1980 can only go from bad to worse.[8]

How shall we then be led? The answer is certainly not through the further imposition of secular bureaucratic planning or more man-made goals and objectives. We are in a crisis of leadership, and the many conflicting caucuses and special interest groups within the church are contributing to that crisis. Our church has begun to operate on all levels much like contemporary society. Everyone and every group is pushing for special consideration and rights, and few if any are willing to give up any of their rights in the interest of a "servant-ministry" for our Lord. Our bishops are elected for life by their lay and clergy peers. I for one am convinced that we are not getting the spiritual and temporal oversight from our bishops that we must have if the church is to be liberated for witness and ministy. Dr. Outler strongly suggests that our bishops ought to assume the leadership which is constitutionally theirs.

The Council of Bishops must actually get on with their constitutional mandate. They, too, are accountable to each successive General Conference—and to the general will of the church. Our bishops might well be reminded that they have been elected by ballot; thus, their authority to oversee derives at the human level from the consent of the overseen. They have been consecrated to be general superintendents of the entire church. . . .

It would be a great day for United Methodism to have a vigorous and effective *episkopē* which by the empowering of God's grace could reach out beyond any local area to oversee the whole church in its whole mission to the whole world.[9]

We do not need more liberal bishops or more conservative bishops. We need bishops who are radically committed as servant-leaders of our Lord Jesus Christ. We do not need leaders who will protect the institution or try to save the church. We do not need leaders who are always in the middle of the road, or sitting on the fence. We need leaders who are willing to risk for Christ's sake, whether that risk be to break new ground and lead new ministries, or to stand for the truth of the faith in the face of the radical onslaught of secularism. We need shepherds and prophets who will lead the church, under the guidance of the Holy Spirit and the Holy Scriptures, and who will not always attempt to measure the pulse of the populace before deciding which way to lead.

Now, I well understand that it is most difficult to be a leader in today's world. That difficulty is no less felt in the church. In the sixties and on through the seventies, all leadership was questioned. I would suggest that the revolt of our young against the traditions and customs of society, including the church, was in many ways instinctively right. The youth, though, in their arrogance and immaturity, corrupted that which might have been instinctively right through a kind of libertine quest for freedom and anarchist attitude toward all authority. The leadership of society and the church tended to react either toward the youth revolt in

101

an authoritative and unbending fashion, or to bend and cower before the judgmental assault of an adolescent revolt. The young people's instincts were right in that there has to be something more than a consumer-oriented culture, growing in affluence, and a search for pleasure and happiness. Their instincts were right in that there must be a greater commitment to peace and a society of justice through caring love than to bombs and missiles as a basis for security in our lives. But their judgments and solutions, in personal morality and in an undisciplined life, as well as in their attack on the socio-economic arena, were often simplistic and immature.

What has happened in the church, as I have observed over the last ten or fifteen years, has been an obsession with the rights and privileges of youth to the point that many leaders are prone to cut and run, rather than stand, even when right is at stake. I have seen impressionable youth used by clever church politicians to stampede a conference or board meeting, when the will of the majority was contravened. How can this happen? Just as no one wants to face the charge of racism, likewise no one wants to be branded as narrow and reactionary, which often occurs if a voice is raised in opposition to a proposal advanced by youth in a meeting. Certainly we should be sensitive to what the young are saying to us, particularly if they are challenging the morality and ethics of society. But, youth are not wise; they haven't lived long enough to lead the church or the country. Is it a symptom of our lack of leadership that our youth seem to intimidate us?

Again the need appears to speak up against the uncritical adulation of youth. It is anomalous that a civilization of long history and great complexity should defer to youth rather than to age. The virtues of youth are the virtues of freshness and vitality, but these are not the virtues that fit one to be the custodian of the culture that society has produced. Deferring to youth is another way of weakening continuity. Mark almost any young person, and you notice that he does not see very much, in the sense of understanding what is present to his vision. He perceives, but he does not interpret, and this is because he is too lacking in those memory traces which lead to ideas and concepts. The memoryless part of mankind cannot be the teachers of culture; they are, however, ready learners of it if the real teachers show faith in the value of what they have.[10]

We desperately need leaders in the church, and teachers of the faith, who will "show faith in the value of what they have." It is my considered judgment that those leaders who have been of the more liberal and secular persuasion have been more ready to provide leadership than have those who are somewhat sympathetic to the more evangelical or traditional interpretations of the gospel. My plea here is, again, that we must have a balanced expression of leadership, which expressly includes the need for personal redemption and personal holiness of heart and life if we are to be truly liberated for witness and ministry. As I express this felt need, I offer my affirmation and respect for those bishops and other leaders who are willing to risk their leadership in taking stands and push for what they believe, even though I may disagree with them greatly.

There is one other area wherein I feel that church leadership is making a significant mistake. If I were to list the prerequisites for approval and success in The United Methodist Church today, I would list loyalty to the system and obedience to the hierarchy. It is almost as if the number one sin of a United Methodist pastor is to question something the church as a whole is doing. Whether a pastor is liberal or conservative, if he or she is reasonably effective, that is, if the church is not dying too fast; if their church pays all the apportionments; if his or her moral behavior is not indiscreet to the point of creating opposition within the congregation; if she or he is a good "gal" or "fellow" and does not rock the boat or make waves, he or she will move ahead in the system.

I realize that what I have said is somewhat overstated, but all pastors will recognize the truth in the position I have taken.

This attitude toward institutional loyalty, as if the institution were God, is in itself a heresy, and is a negative influence on ministry in the church. It has caused many pastors to give in to the system, to settle into a lack-luster career, and forget the high calling of God which brought them into the ordained ministry. John Wesley had a definitive word to say about this matter.

We act at all times on one plain uniform principle—we will obey the rulers and governors of the Church, whenever we can consistently with our duty to God, whenever we cannot, we will quietly obey God rather than men. [11]

Some of us have this same commitment, in the pattern of Wesley and Luther, wherein we believe that our church and its leadership are not being responsive to the biblical faith and the leading of the Holy Spirit. We, too, must speak and risk for our Lord and the faith we hold. With the Holy Scripture as the primary foundation of our faith and practice and with the guidance and direction of the Holy Spirit as our teacher and guide, we must dare to speak the truth as we understand it. I am prepared to listen and dialogue with those who disagree, but speak I must even though I do so with some trepidation.

There is one other matter concerning the leadership of our church, particularly the bishops of the church. The election of the episcopacy has become so politicized and the process so structured that it is highly unlikely that an avowed evangelical will be elected in the near future. In the past several quadrenniums there has been a tendency to elect as bishops staff members of general boards and agencies, college or seminary administrators, or persons in conference administration. The persons most likely to be nominated and elected are those who have a long history of loyalty to the system, who have not been controversial, and who have paid the price of being steady churchmen or churchwomen, without any apparent evidence of being set in their convictions, faith, or doctrine. In other words they must be open to the process of continual change and be malleable cogs for the system.

It was interesting to note the comments of several of the new bishops elected in 1980. There was a tendency to affirm a firm commitment to the broad and undefinable middle ground of faith and polity. One might hope that occasionally a bishop would not be afraid to offer a radical commitment to Jesus Christ as personal Savior and Lord—as well as a radical commitment to holiness of heart and life including justice in society. Frankly, I cannot imagine John Wesley or Martin Luther being concerned that their colleagues and followers be assured that they were in the middle, but never radical one way or another.

With the recommendation in the *Discipline* that 60 percent of those voting in the Jurisdictional Conference must vote for a candidate for bishop to insure election—66 percent in the North Central Jurisdiction—a determined minority can thwart the will of the majority. It has been my observation over the last twenty years that the liberal more secularly oriented clergy and lay delegates are more determined and resolute in their support of a candidate than either the more evangelical or moderate institutionalists. In many cases they have been able to block potentially strong leaders with whom they disagree and finally to win the marathon of endurance by holding out the longest.

The practice of going to Jurisdictional Conference and making a swap for delegate votes for your candidate, on the most favorable basis possible, smacks of the cynical practices in the public political arena. Technically and pragmatically the delegates do have a secret ballot. The pressure is very great, however, to bind yourself to one candidate, and swap your vote to another, in order to insure success. This does not enable the individual delegate to be freely led by the Holy

Spirit and cast his or her ballot according to honest conviction. Somehow, there must be developed a more open election process, one that takes pluralism seriously, so there can be a balance in the Council of Bishops. We must have a balanced and effective leadership to which a majority of the church will respond and follow in witness and ministry. Surely all of us agree that we must do something to enable more grass-roots trust and confidence in the hierarchy and leadership of the church.

VIII

The Recovery of Covenant Trust

One of the significant problems facing the church today is the credibility gap that exists between the grass-roots church and the leadership and programs of our national boards and agencies. Anyone who does not recognize that there is a low level of trust at the local level for those on the national level must surely have his head in the sand. Countless pastors, out of basic institutional loyalty and concern for their own future in ministry, continue to urge their laity to support fully the institutional church in all its apportionments, askings, and programs. Many do this in spite of basic disagreement with and misgivings about the nature of some of the programs and the mind-set of many of the leaders. Were it not for this basic institutional loyalty of those in the pastorate, support for the mission and program of the church would have diminished far more than it has. Many of us feel that we can support most of the programs and projects of the general boards and agencies, and we have not wanted to encourage distrust and possible revolt against the worldwide mission and ministry of the church. Too many of our laypeople are parochial in their understanding and commitments and would too readily forsake their responsibility as disciples of Christ to support the worldwide mission of the church.

The leadership of the national church is skillful in using the pressure and obligation for institutional loyalty to maintain support for its programs, while evidencing very little respect for the concerns and opinions of local leaders. It is my opinion, based on my own experience as a local pastor, church administrator, and general board executive, that many of the people in national leadership roles have a certain "messianic complex" about who they are and what they are doing. Many of them actually believe that they know what is best for the church and have no basic hesitancy at all to plan and implement programs that they know perhaps do not have the support of their constituency. In my considered judgment this mind-set must be increasingly challenged, for those who lead must accept for themselves the role of "servant-leaders," rather than wielders of power who take for granted the presumption that they have the responsibility and right to make decisions for those they consider "less wise" and "less knowledgeable."

Personally, I have come to the place where I choose no longer to "protect" the laity from the truth about some of the attitudes, positions, and programs of much of our national leadership. I choose to trust the laity with an open and honest look at the direction and mind-set of the church leadership, and I hope to challenge them to deal responsibly in their decisions as committed disciples of Jesus Christ. I recognize that there is some risk of further weakening the trust and loyalty of the grass-roots church in the institution. I do not see any options, however, for those of my persuasion other than to take the risk. The alternative is to forsake conviction and allow the bureaucracy of the church to continue in a direction that basically ignores legitimate spiritual and evangelical concerns. And, this is what the bureaucracy will continue to do, as long as we express only mildly our disagreement and continue to support the system with our money. Now please put what I am saying within the context of the record of my ministry. For over twenty-five years, the churches which I have pastored have faithfully supported all the programs of the church. I hope to continue to give that kind of loyal support. But I am no longer willing to do it quietly, since I believe that the leadership of the national church is not truly open to a more evangelical and holistic approach toward the gospel. In other words, for me the time has come and gone when I am willing to be smiled at benevolently and essentially told that my responsibility is to pay for and support the system, no matter how much I disagree with what is being done.

The national leadership of the church, especially our bishops, must begin to be more open to evangelical leadership and concerns or they will preside over an ever-weakening church, with an increasing loss of trust and support at the grass-roots level.

And, now, to get at some of the specifics. It has been general knowledge in the church among those who are familiar with the former Board of Missions and its successor, the General Board of Global Ministries, that the staff leadership of the board has essentially frozen out or refused to consider for placement many missionaries who are primarily concerned with evangelistic or evangelical priorities. This has been done irrespective of the wishes of at least some of the national leadership of the overseas churches involved. I know of one young couple who are open and inclusive in their witness and ministry, having exemplified this in their own lives by adopting an ethnic child. This young couple failed to pass the screening of the general board under the guise that they were not politically and socially sensitive. At the same time I was aware, through personal friendship with the bishop of the country involved, that the local national leadership of that church did not want missionaries who were primarily concerned with fomenting social and political revolution. They wanted missionaries who would come and help them build up the church. I am personally aware of this because the bishop of that church shared with me intimately and gave me a copy of a letter that he sent to the general board. I include the whole letter here, because it reflects the concern of some national leaders who do not desire to have our general boards assume the responsibility for having as their number one priority the making or changing of social, economic, or political policy in their country.

January 26, 1971

Dear Brothers and co-laborers in Christ:

After discussing at some length the use of Missionary personnel in the recently inaugurated Methodist Church of Peru, we write to you about a concern we have concerning the qualities desired in future personnel recommended for service in Peru.

In view of the developing stage of our church in Peru, which is yet a young church with an urgent need for broadening the base of our total mission here, we feel the need for missionaries who can openly and honestly identify with the evangelistic message and mission of the church as well as serve the community with their special talents and personal witness.

We are not attempting to say that we want "pietistic" missionaries; but neither do we want missionaries who cannot honestly identify with the evangelistic efforts of the church which are needed for an outgoing total ministry in any given local church as well as for a base for a growing mission to the Peruvian people.

We feel that some missionaries assigned to Peru in recent years have reacted negatively to the Peruvian Church because of a basic conflict at this point. We understand that the current religious scene in the U.S.A. is considerably different from that of Peru and therefore we cannot assume that a person who responds well to some concepts of ministry will be able to make that ministry in and through the Peruvian Church.

Specialists will be needed who are competent in their area of concern, but we want that they also be a vital part of our church in its formative years here, and we would like to avoid the negative reactions which have been felt and openly declared by some fraternal workers ("Missionaries") among us. Prophets we need; but if they are to be true prophets they need to identify themselves with the Church that they seek to reform or renew.

We recognize the right of individuals to differ in doctrine and personal preference but we reject the concept that a missionary sent as a fraternal worker need not have a personal Christian witness nor needs to associate with the worshipping community represented by the Church.

We also expect to have some personal information on prospective personnel and have an exchange of letters with them prior to their assignment to Peru, in order that there might be a more favorable climate of acceptation on the part of both the Peruvian Church and the prospective missionary.

> Respectfully submitted,
> f. National Committee on Coordination
>   The Methodist Church of Peru,

Original signed by:
Wenceslao Bahamonde, Elton Watlington, Ismael Fernandez
Bishop

When the board would not send missionaries acceptable to the church in Peru, some of us took the responsibility, at the request of the church in Peru, to send this young couple to be interviewed by the national leadership of the church there. At the request of the Peruvian church leadership, we then funded this young couple who were placed on special appointment and allowed to work with the Peruvian church in an arrangement negotiated between leaders of the local conference and the church in Peru. This is but one of many similar instances which could be used to illustrate the issue involved.

It is well known indeed that the leadership of our board is strongly critical of the United States government which they consider to be acting in a colonial or imperialistic manner toward Third-World countries. Let us assume that they are sometimes right in their criticism. What is indeed strange and indefensible is that they often act toward the national church leadership in exactly the same colonial or imperial manner which they condemn in the U.S. government. Again, let me make it clear that I personally know of other situations where such actions have occurred. It is my conviction, based on my own knowledge and observation of the deployment of missionary personnel in the last decade or so, that it is the basic philosophy of the World Division to have as their primary objective the changing of social, economic, and political structures in the countries where they are involved. Insofar as many of the staff leaders are concerned, to talk about the great commission or to lead people to faith in Jesus Christ is to be irrelevant to the age in which we live and thoroughly outmoded and outdated in theology. This stance or mind-set is far more ideological in nature than theological.

This leads me to raise some very serious questions for United Methodists to consider. Does the basic leadership of the General Board of Global Ministries, and including especially the Women's Division, have a holistic approach to the gospel which enables a balanced witness and ministry inclusive of personal salvation as well as social change and witness? Is there any justifiable evidence that there is a political and economic policy bias that endorses or promotes some form of leftist or collectivist model as the Christian choice for today? Has there been reflected in the promotional and study literature a balanced critical analysis, or has there been an almost carte blanche approval of the societies that have developed, say in Cuba, as well as in other Marxist states? I for one do not believe that the boards and agencies referred to above have promoted a balanced and whole gospel and have not, therefore, been authentically representative of the biblical faith. I am also convinced that there is a political and economic bias, represented in staff and program, which is basically in support of the collectivist state as the answer to the betterment of society. I suppose that one should not be especially surprised at this trend, considering the basic theological and psychological presuppositions that have been the foundation for much of modern thought and cultural analysis. After all, if we are not dependent on a transcendent God to redeem us and change our lives; if we are, as human beings self-actualizing and autonomous, responsible on our own to fashion and create a good society, then the state is the natural replacement for God in dealing with all ethics and morality. This is a basic mistake which much of the leadership of the church in the modern era has made. In turning away from the authority and lordship of God in our lives, including the authority of Scripture for faith and morals, it is an almost axiomatic next step to move to some form of statism, which supposedly will be the protector of justice and the guide in faith and morals. In this sense, the more secular liberation theologies make the same mistake that the moral majority often makes; that is, that they have the right through the power of the state to coerce the public to accept their own economic or social views. The danger should be apparent from either direction, if the extremes of either are realized: the danger of tyranny of the left or the right.

Before I go on to document some of the evidence and reasons for the position I am taking, let me clearly indicate my own conviction that no Christian should equate the Christian faith with one form of government or economic order. Our loyalty, as disciples of Jesus Christ, must be in a singular fashion to God and His will and direction for our lives. All economic and political orders with which I am familiar fall short of being pleasing to God and being providers of justice for all. This certainly has been true, even of our own form of republican democracy, wherein certain segments of our society, particularly the ethnic minorities have been the subject of prejudice, intolerance, and injustice. We do have constitutional provisions to protect the rights of the individual and the minority, but they have not always worked. Therefore, we should be continuously involved in and committed to working for a more just society. Also, history has taught us that an unbridled and unchecked laissez-faire capitalism is often brutal and uncaring toward those who do not have the power to protect themselves.

The economic order in most Western democracies has been primarily under the formative guidance of the Protestant work ethic and has essentially followed some form of free enterprise capitalism in the economic order. It is perhaps a true irony that Protestantism has taken seriously the sinful nature of man, the notion that humanity is basically prone to self-will and self-interest, has adopted an economic theory that recognizes it, and has been largely successful in the production of goods and services in the fulfillment of that self-interest. It ought to be more clearly seen than it is how such an economic order can become the victim of consumerism, to the extreme of selfish affluence which characterizes much of the West. I for one would certainly agree that there has been exploitation and injustice fostered by the greed of economic gain and advantage, all in the name of freedom and free enterprise. It has been necessary for labor to organize to protect its own rights and for laws to be enacted to protect the public interest as well as to protect individual and minority rights. All of these matters are of legitimate concern to Christians who take seriously the commandment to love their neighbor as themselves.

After admitting and affirming certain ills and problems in the economic system known as capitalism, wouldn't it be logical then to favor some form of collectivist or socialist state as the right expression of Christian faith? In the first place, the basic form of the socialist state in our era has been nontheistic or Godless in its expression and hopelessly utopian in its attitude toward humanity and society. In addition it has been more oppressive of individual and minority rights than any of the Western democracies. The continued desire of many intellectuals and minorities to flee from the oppression of the collectivist states is ample evidence of their failure to provide a truly human society. Finally, even in those countries where the socialist or collectivist system has been tried and where freedom of faith and the practice of one's religion is allowed, the collectivist economic system has not worked to provide adequate goods and services for the benefit of society. It should be obvious that human beings do produce more for themselves and others in freedom than they produce under coercion and control. It is here that the Christian theology of stewardship and benevolence toward one's neighbor must be practiced, preached, and taught by the church. I am completely convinced that a better life, spiritually, socially, and economically can be provided in some model of democratically guided free market economy than can or ever will be provided in a collectivist or socialist state. I also recognize that one can be a Christian and take a different view than I hold.

The real question is, Do the national and staff leaders of our church have the right to hold and foster a view favoring some form of collectivist economic order as being *the* Christian answer? Further, is it an act of disloyalty for a member of the church to raise questions, particularly when the view held has no specific sanction in Scripture and is probably in contradiction to the view and will of a sizable majority of the church? There is some indication that national church leadership looks on all questions raised and on any alternative directions in policy or mission program as being subversive, disloyal, and counterproductive to the life and mission of the church. It seems to me that at times national church leaders, including some bishops, are almost pathological in their reaction to any serious questioning of official church programs or activities of any national leaders. Nevertheless, there is an increasing conviction on the part of many pastors and laity, in the tradition of John Wesley and Martin Luther, that loyalty to God and the Scriptures must be placed above any attempt to compel or insist on loyalty to the institution as being supreme. Therefore, we who seriously disagree with many of the actions and positions of our general boards and agencies and are seriously concerned about the lack of more spiritual and evangelical leadership of our bishops, must raise our voices, or else deny what we are convinced is the leading of the Holy Spirit in our lives.

I expect that many of the leaders of our church disagree, not only with my own economic convictions, but also with my charge of a bias toward state collectivism on the part of many persons in staff leadership of our boards and agencies. Those who are familiar with the national and international bureaucracies of the church surely know that there is evidence for the position I am taking. In a recent article in *The Christian Century*, Dr. Peter Berger, professor of sociology at Boston College, speaks of the danger of the religious political right and the religious political left in our nation today. He says, speaking of the "recent upsurge of the Christian right,"

Politically, what is most troubling is the effortless linkage between reactionary religion and reactionary politics, especially in terms of an aggressive and at least potentially bellicose nationalism. Flag-waving preachers are always disturbing; they become truly frightening in an age of nuclear weapons. The alarm provoked by the Christian New Right, then, is not unreasonable.

Inevitably, however, the religiopolitical extravaganza on the right has reminded fair-minded observers of the comparable extravaganza on the left—a phenomenon which, far from having been laid to rest with the late 1960s, is still going full blast and has even been institutionalized in important agencies of mainline religion in this country. Inevitably, one must ask by what criteria one deems good the pronouncements of left-of-center geese while condemning the preachments of right-of-center ganders. . . .

If it is wrong to sanctify Americanism in Christian terms, how about the virulent *anti*-Americanism that permeates Christian church agencies and seminaries? Why is flag-*waving* objectionable, while flag-*burning* was an admirable expression of the prophetic ministry of the church?

Dr. Berger concludes that

the church does *not* have the competence to bless any particular political modality either practiced or proposed as an alternative. And it is precisely in failing to make this distinction that American churches have gone astray, on both sides of the political spectrum.[1]

Dr. Berger's charge that in many "important agencies of mainline religion in this country" left-of-center political bias has been institutionalized is supported by certain evidence from within the boards and agencies of The United Methodist Church.

At the 1980 General Conference, a layman from Maryland brought to the Conference a "white paper" entitled: "Preliminary Inquiry Regarding Financial Contributions to Outside Political Groups by Boards and Agencies of The United Methodist Church, 1977-1979."[2] David Jessup is not any right-wing extremist or member of the moral majority as some would like to brand him. It would have been easier for the establishment if he could have been so identified. No, this concerned layman is a special assistant to the Committee on Political Education of the AFL-CIO. Let me quote a paragraph from the introduction to the paper which explains how Mr. Jessup got involved in his inquiry.

My interest in the political orientation of the Methodist Church began when my wife and I started to attend services at Marvin Memorial Methodist Church in 1977 not long after moving to the Washington, D.C., area from the West Coast. My wife is a Family Nurse Practitioner whose grandfather was a Methodist minister. I am employed by the AFL-CIO. We had been active in the Peace Corps in Peru, and in the civil rights and farm workers movements in California, and we were interested in becoming involved in church related projects such as refugee assistance. When my children brought home Sunday school appeals for wheat shipments to the government of Vietnam, and the controversy over Methodist support for the Patriotic Front in Zimbabwe became public, I was troubled, but not persuaded that these projects represented anything more than minor aberrations from a more consistent tradition of Methodist support for democratic values. After several visits to the Methodist Building near the U.S. Capitol, and several months of research on the political orientation of groups receiving church funds, I am no longer so certain.[3]

It has been interesting to observe the response of the church leadership to the "Jessup" paper. A rather extensive paper was prepared in response to the concerns raised by Mr. Jessup by United Methodist Communications in cooperation with the Board of Global Ministries and Board of Church and Society. *Newscope* gave extensive coverage, and Bishop Roy Nichols responded as the president of the Council of Bishops. It is obvious that the leadership understands the possible serious repercussions that could result from an increasing public awareness of the questions raised in the "Jessup report." It is not as obvious that they are willing to consider any possible error or bias in their support of specific causes or to consider seriously a change in direction.

Let us look at the stance of the World Division and the Women's Divison toward the Castro government in Cuba. Jessup pointed out that the World Division made an $18,000 grant to the Cuba Resource Center in 1978. The official response of the church under date of October 17, 1980, in describing the Cuba Resource Center was as follows:

Cuba Resource Center was established by Roman Catholic and Protestant Latin Americans to provide religious communications with an accurate description of the Cuban revolution, to promote communication between North Americans and Cubans, and to counter U.S. and church policies which contribute to injustice with regard to Cuba and Latin America. CRC met the Latin American policy guidelines of the World Division. CRC was disbanded in 1979 and subsequently re-established with a different scope.[4]

What the facts provided by the church didn't reveal is the general tenor and direction of the so-called "accurate" description of the Cuban revolution.

Center coordinator Mary Lou Sahor praises the "new dignity" and "more human existence" of the Cuban people under communism. She notes appreciation for the help of the Soviet Union, without which "Cuba could not have grown in domestic stability or international prestige. The island nation has been adopted as a symbol of revolutionary hope and courage by the Third World, and has the long term support of a country (the USSR) which does not seek economic domination in the form of trade agreements."[5]

One would suppose that the "new dignity" and "more human existence" of the Cuban people under communism was not a part of the consideration when tens of thousands of Cubans fled their homeland recently for refuge in the United States and other countries. The Cuban Resource Center may have met the guidelines of the World Division, but if it did, many of us are convinced that the guidelines are in error and should be changed.

With regard to the Women's Division and its School of Christian Mission in the summer of 1980, the pro-Cuban collectivist bias is clear. The assigned text declares that the Cuban Revolution

has concretely and historically inaugurated a series of values in human relations that make it possible for the whole of modern technical scientific development to be at the service of the full dignity of the human person. . . . Cubans are the only Latin Americans who have broken with dependent capitalism and its accompanying dehumanization of the common people. The revolutionary government established a socialist society that focused national priorities on the needs of the people instead of those multi-national corporations.[6]

One might conclude from the assigned text of the School of Christian Mission in 1980 that the Cuban revolution and establishment of a socialist state had enhanced the "full dignity of the human race" and perhaps brought in the kingdom of God for the Cuban people.

The story continues with the summer issue, 1981, of *Common Ground*, a newsletter of the United Methodist Voluntary Service. The frontispiece of the booklet is entitled "Cuba: A Land of Contrasts," with a laudatory story about the Cuban revolution beginning on page fourteen. Cuba is pictured as a land which has solved all its problems.

Now, in a remarkable short time, Cuba has eliminated illiteracy, raised life expectancy to one of the highest in the world, provided universal, free preventive health and medical care, reduced unemployment to well below that of most Western industrialized societies, and virtually eliminated institutional racism and sexism.[7]

Cuba is contrasted with the United States of America, with Cuba pointing the way for us to handle our problems.

Cuba, before the revolution, contained most of the conditions that so many poor communities in the U.S. now confront. Cuba today demonstrates a radically different way of solving the problems underlying those conditions. Indeed, Cuba represents a vision of the future shared by many poor and working people in the U.S. today. Knowing what the revolution has brought and what it has cost, is an immensely important challenge for people seriously committed to bringing change to the United States.

What made it possible for Cuba to make these changes while the U.S. cannot?[8]

The so-called "democracy" of Cuba is pictured as providing a way to eliminate powerlessness and hopelessness among the people.

We learned how arrogant it appears to others that the United States government, which cannot provide adequately for its own citizens, presumes to advise another people how they should plan their future. We learned about the narrow (and incorrect) perspective we have been taught about democracy—that because we have a "two-party" system no other can be democratic. We learned that apathy, so prevalent in our country, is virtually non-existent in today's Cuba, where powerlessness and hopelessness no longer prevail. We learned that national decision-makers can admit their mistakes, and rather than lose face or influence, can gain people's trust when they are willing to make the changes the people recommend.[9]

I suppose one could conclude from the above that after twenty years of the Cuban revolution the over one hundred thousand Cubans who fled to the United States in 1980 did so because Cuban society had been changed according to their wishes. Surely anyone who romanticizes life in a Marxist state as being free and prosperous is not a serious student of history.

One wonders if the leaders of our national church have ever read any of the writings of the Russian dissidents, those who have lived the longest in the collectivist state, Russia, which is the patron and model of Cuba today. In a collection of essays published in a book entitled *From Under the Rubble*, Alexander Solzhenitsyn and six of his colleagues courageously, with devastating analysis and exposure, present the cruel face of a society based on a false humanism and state collectivism. Alexander Solzhenitsyn says:

In no socialist doctrine, however, are moral demands seen as the essence of socialism—there is merely a promise that morality will fall like manna from heaven after the socialization of property. . . . But in the great expanse of our collectivized countryside, where people always and only lived by labor and had no other interest in life but labor, it is only under "socialism" that labor has become an accursed burden from which men flee. Let us add to this that throughout our broad country and along its roads the heaviest manual labor is performed by women, since the men moved onto machines or into administration. . . .

Our present system is unique in world history, because over and above its physical and economic constraints, it demands of us total surrender of our souls, continuous and active participation in the general, conscious lie. To this putrefaction of the soul, this spiritual enslavement, human beings who wish to be human cannot consent. When Caesar, having exacted what is Caesar's, demands still more insistently that we render unto him what is God's—that is a sacrifice we dare not make![10]

In an essay entitled "Contemporary Socioeconomic Systems and Their Future Prospects," Mikhail Agursky says:

Socialism consciously rejects spiritual and moral values, it preaches violence as the means of social struggle, thereby arriving at a negation of the concept of social justice which it advances. . . . The Marxist theory of the class struggle has become not a means of defending the workers' interest but an ideology to justify terror and hegemony over them.[11]

Under the pseudonym A.B., the hope of Christianity is held out as the only answer to the tyranny of collectivist oppression. A.B. says:

Mysteriously and unsuspected by the busy multitudes, Christian consciousness, once almost defunct, is stealing back. . . . It is as if a door had opened while nobody was looking. Why is this rebirth taking place in our country, where Christianity is attacked particularly systematically and with great brutality, while the rest of the world suffers a general decline in faith and religious feeling? . . . We have passed through such bottomless pits, . . . we have experienced such utter exhaustion of human resources that we have learned to see the "one essential" that cannot be taken away from man, and we have learned not to look to human resources for succor. In glorious destitution, in utter defenselessness in the face of suffering, our hearts have been kindled by an inner spiritual warmth and have opened to new, unexpected impulses. . . . We are profoundly convinced that Christianity alone possesses enough motive force gradually to inspire and transform our world.[12]

Just as there was a blindness for many years, and still is for some today, about the heart and face of the collectivist state in Russia, so there is a similar blindness about the state in Cuba, Angola, China, and other countries patterned after the same models. To try to brush this bias or "blindness" under the rug, using the rubric that we sometimes must join hands even with those with whom we disagree in order to help the poor and the oppressed, will not wash with the church public, and will further cripple the church unless the issue is dealt with more honestly.

There are any number of other examples of support or endorsement that would indicate a clear bias of influential leadership in the General Board of Global Ministries and the Women's Division for a collectivist-socialistic form of economy and government as opposed to any sanction of a free market economy and government modeled on the Western democratic tradition. In a free society, persons certainly have the right to such a view, but there is this question, Does such a collectivist economy and authoritative government truly advance freedom and the good for society? Is there any warrant to support such a position as "the" Christian answer? I for one say, unequivocally, no! Further, I am convinced that a vast majority of my fellow United Methodist Christians agree with the position I am stating. If so, what do we have to do to effect a change? And, does the national leadership of the church have the right to contravene the will of the majority of the church?

We may be a long way from finding consensus and final agreement concerning the issues I have raised. It is imperative that we begin to work at finding that consensus in a more fair and democratic fashion or The United Methodist Church will suffer irreparable harm. We do not have a covenant trust relationship at this time, and the lay members of the church are being crippled in witness and ministry. We are in a time of crisis, and I earnestly plead with the bishops of our church to give spiritual and pastoral leadership to the church rather than to allow the church to be dominated by a bureaucratized structure which is not responsive to the membership it is called to serve.

effort in talking to many of my fellow pastors and to many laypersons during the past several years urging them to remain active in The United Methodist Church. There are several reasons why I remain a United Methodist and why I believe there is great hope for change and renewal of witness and ministry in our church. Some of those reasons are as follows. First, our church has a great tradition of solid evangelical theology and commitment to historic Christianity. Second, Methodism has always reflected a biblical concern for social justice and involved concern for the dispossessed and hungry of the world. Third, we have always been in the forefront of a genuine "catholic" tradition, serving as a significant supporter and leader in ecumenical endeavors. Finally, we have the tradition of a free pulpit and strong support in that tradition for a prophetic ministry. I know of no other denomination that combines all of these elements so well as The United Methodist Church.

For over twenty-five years now I have had the privilege to serve as a minister of the gospel of Jesus Christ within The United Methodist Church. It is here that I hope to serve my Lord so long as I am physically and spiritually able to be an effective pastor-teacher within the faith. It is my conviction that the wind of the Spirit is blowing across the church in these days, and there has never been a time of greater opportunity to reach others for Jesus Christ and build up the church for witness and ministry. This can be done ultimately only on the local level. In the final analysis, renewal has never begun with structure and never will. The Reformation and the Wesleyan Revival were both grass-roots movements, not centered in the hierarchy of the church. Instead they were movements of the people in response to the wind of the Spirit which came from God to renew and reform His church. That same God is still in control. God is bringing new life to His people at the grass-roots level today. It is a great thrill and joy to be a part of that, in spite of my own serious concerns about the structure and leadership of the church on the national level. I am committed to continue to be a part of what God is doing to renew, reform, and empower His church in today's world. It is my hope that such renewal can and will come in leadership and structure; but if not, God will bypass both the structure and those in authority and raise up other structures and leaders to serve and lead, as He has done countless times before. Renewal is occurring in many local churches across our land, where the Word of God is preached and taught and where people are open to the life-changing power of God's Spirit in their lives. Only such churches will be able to serve the needs of their own members and grow in vital Christian witness and ministry. Our people must be equipped with God's love, the power of the Holy Spirit, and the gifts of His Spirit if they are to be both flexible and bold enough to reach modern secular humanity for Jesus Christ. Thanks be unto God! This is possible!

PART TWO

*The
Church in
Action*

IX

Equipped for Ministry

There is one body and one Spirit, just as also you were called in one hope of your calling; one Lord, one faith, one baptism, one God and Father of all who is over all and through all and in all. But to each one of us grace was given according to the measure of Christ's gift. . . . And He gave some as apostles, and some as prophets, and some as evangelists, and some as pastors and teachers, for the equipping of the saints for the work of service, to the building up of the body of Christ; until we all attain to the unity of the faith, and of the knowledge of the Son of God, to a mature man, to the measure of the stature which belongs to the fulness of Christ. (Eph. 4:4-7, 11-13)

The teaching of the Apostle Paul recorded in Ephesians 4 has been a pivotal factor in my ministry for nearly twenty years. Not only do we have one Lord, one faith, and one baptism, we also have one God and Father of us all, who is over all, and through all, and in all. The truth of Paul's affirmation is one of the greatest strengths and comforts of my life. For if God is over all, and active through all the events of our lives, and is present in our lives at all times, then we always live in a time of resurrection possibility. As we trust God enough and actively have faith in His promises, He will liberate His Church for witness and ministry. Whatever the structure, and however weak or strong the leadership may be in any given moment, our hope is in our God who is everlasting in His love and steadfast and sure in His mercy.

The gifts of the Spirit as enumerated in the fourth chapter of Ephesians have been called the equipping gifts, or the servant-leadership gifts. They are provided by the Holy Spirit to enable or properly equip all the people of God to do the work of Christ's ministry. A proper theology of these enabling or equipping gifts and an obedience to this teaching of Scripture is imperative to any liberation of the church for witness and ministry. Persons who have accepted the role of leadership in the church, whether ordained or lay, must come to an understanding of the role of the Holy Spirit in equipping them for their calling. I have used the word *calling* intentionally instead of vocation, career, or profession. For I am convinced that a person should not become or accept a leadership role in the church without the confirming witness of God's Spirit and the proper equipping by the Spirit for the ministry to which one is called. Then, those of us·who respond to God's call to servant-ministry, must clearly understand that we are to lead, equip, confirm, motivate, and be with all of our people in ministry. We must again recapture the scriptural and Reformation model of the priesthood of all believers, with the profound and essential understanding that all who follow Christ as Savior and Lord are called into His ministry of witness and service.

We in the ordained ministry have too long allowed ourselves to be separated, or "elevated" into the model of professional ministers who do the ministry of the church. Perhaps we have even liked this to some degree, because it has given us an edge over our laity and set us apart with a certain status. Essentially several things are wrong and harmful in this model of ministry. First, it is not in accordance with the teaching of the Scripture and not in keeping with the model of servant-leader as patterned by Christ. Second, it is impossible for any one human being to do all the needed ministry in any congregation or church family. Finally, it allows the laity of the church to escape and abandon the calling that God places on them to be active disciples of Jesus Christ themselves. All of us are called into active servant-ministry for our Lord, and this includes the laity.

Let me digress here for just a moment and consider the ministry as a profession, say, in comparison to medicine and law. Doctors practice medicine or perform surgery, but their patients are not being trained to be doctors. Lawyers practice law for their clients, but their clients are not being trained to be lawyers. Not so with pastors and teachers—who are called to equip all the people of God for work in His ministry. There is a place, seminary, for training the ordained clergy, and that has some clear analogy to the school of law or medicine for training lawyers and doctors. But, here, the likeness ends, for the role of the pastor-teacher with his or her parishioners is different, because we are not called to practice theology as a profession. No, we are called to live the faith and, through preaching, teaching, and example among our laity, to enable them to say yes to their ministry and to live out their faith as servant-disciples of our Lord in all the arenas of their lives. But such enabling is not being effectively done in most congregations. As a result those churches are limping along with a caretaker ministry for its members, and the call to go into the world and give their lives as reconcilers and ambassadors is not being heard and followed. The call to active discipleship is not being prophetically made by most of us who have been given the privilege to be pastors and teachers.

This is surely one of the areas of greatest weakness in the training of ordained clergy. Very few pastors I have known give any significant time to their responsibility to be teaching elders. In turn, the teaching role of the district superintendent and the bishop is seldom seriously attempted, perhaps due to an endless claim on the time of both to be involved in administration and in attending countless church meetings. I suspect, however, that the primary reason is that we have not been trained to be teachers to our laity—especially teachers of the Scripture. While I recognize that seminaries are not Bible colleges, I am convinced that far too little time is spent in the study of Scripture in seminary training. Most of the training in hermeneutics is rational and critical in nature, and does not really prepare us to come before the Scripture and allow the Holy Spirit to lead us in teaching our people. Most pastors, if they teach at all, follow the pattern or attitude that they learned in seminary. By this I mean that they approach the Scriptures primarily rationally and critically and explain away far too much the miraculous and transcendental. Most of us are not willing to come before the Word with the necessary openness so that the One who inspired the Word can lead us into the truth provided in Scripture. However, I have seen many people come to a saving and mature knowledge of Jesus Christ when the Word of God was regularly opened and taught with reverence and obedience. The Scripture tells what the Spirit will do:

"But the Helper, the Holy Spirit, whom the Father will send in My name, He will teach you all things, and bring to your remembrance all that I have said to you." (John 14:26)

"But when He, the Spirit of truth, comes, He will guide you into all the truth; for He will not speak on His own initiative, but whatever He hears, He will speak; and He will disclose to you what is to come. He shall glorify Me; for He shall take of Mine, and shall disclose it to you." (John 16:13-14)

Until we who are called to be pastors and teachers become devoted disciples and students of the Word of God in our own meditation and study, we cannot lead our people and teach them what God and the church has ordained us to do.

The *Discipline* spells out in some detail the duties of a pastor. The order of duties as listed in the *Discipline* is indeed indicative of the primary importance of the study of Scripture to the life of a Christian and of a congregation.

Duties of a Pastor—Pastors are responsible for ministering to the needs of the whole community as well as to the needs of the people of their charge, equipping them to fulfill their ministry to each other and to the world to which they are sent as servants under the lordship of Christ. Among the pastor's duties are the following:

a) To preach the Word, read and teach the Scriptures, and engage the people in study and witness.[1] (Paragraph 438.2*a*)

To meet their needs and to equip them for service—as pastor and teacher—this is the command of God and the order of the church. And, the foundation of all that we do in fulfilling this command and order is to preach and teach the Word. Quite frankly too little preaching today is of and from the Word, and even less is done in fulfilling the mandate to teach the Word. This is surely one of the crisis points in the failure of leadership in the church today. And, yet, if the Bible is to be truly our guide for faith and action, as surely it must be, then we who are called by God to give pastoral leadership to the church must make a primary investment of our lives in ministry to teaching the Word of God to our people. The church can go on without committees, boards, meetings, and such, but the church will not survive as the church of Jesus Christ unless the Word of Scripture is taught by those called to lead.

We must come again to the place of the psalmist:

Thy word I have treasured in my heart,
That I may not sin against Thee.
Blessed art Thou, O Lord;
Teach me Thy statutes.
With my lips I have told of
All the ordinances of Thy mouth.

I have rejoiced in the way of Thy testimonies,
As much as in all riches.
I will meditate on Thy precepts,
And regard Thy ways.
I shall delight in Thy statutes;
I shall not forget Thy word. . . .
How sweet are Thy words to my taste!
Yes, sweeter than honey to my mouth! . . .
Thy word is a lamp to my feet,
And a light to my path.

(Ps. 119:11-16, 103, 105)

If we are to cease stumbling in the darkness as pastors and shepherds in the church, the Word of God must again become a lamp unto our feet and to the feet of our people. When we are willing to obediently come before God's Word again and live obediently to what it teaches, we shall be liberated for witness and ministry. Truly the Word of God is the "bread of life" for the Christian.

If the Word of God is the "bread of life" and a lamp unto our feet, then fellowship with God in prayer and devotion is the breath of life for the Christian. I learned this most important truth fifteen years ago when I was a pastor of a growing suburban church. Coming in from a long day one evening about ten o'clock, I found myself confessing to my wife that though I was helping a lot of people get their lives back together, going to a lot of meetings, and keeping the church running, I seemed to be coming apart at the seams myself.

Just at that time I received a call from a parishioner with whom I had been counseling about marriage problems, greatly aggravated by the alcoholism of her husband. He had agreed to see me, and they wanted me to come over at once. Since we had been hoping and praying for this breakthrough for some time, and since he might not want to see me the next day, I retied my shoes and tie and left for their home about

10:30 P.M. I felt good about the session, but when I returned home about midnight, I still knew that I was coming apart at the seams and running out of resources for my own life.

Then about two hours later I was wakened by a call from a former business associate who was in trouble and desperately needed my help. He too was struggling with alcoholism. I went down to his hotel and found myself trying to give a man, hungry and thirsty for the water of life, a drink of that water from my own glass which was empty. Somehow, I knew, with an oughtness that was impelling, that something had to change or I would go under. Oh, to all outward appearances I was a great success. My congregation was growing and I was "going up" in the ministry, but, I was going under in my own heart and soul. As I went to sleep that night, I found myself saying to God, "You had better do something or I have had it! I cannot go on like this!"

The next morning, about 5:30 A.M., I awakened and could not go back to sleep. I literally cried out to God, "I asked you to do something in my life! Please, at least, let me sleep!" I have not heard the voice of God many times in my life as clearly as I heard it then. Oh, not audibly so someone else could have heard it, but very much the voice of God saying, "Ira, if I am to help you—get UP!—and spend some time with ME! I am the rest you need!" And so, I got up and began to develop slowly and sometimes falteringly a pattern of prayer, devotion, and study at the beginning of each day. I could not go on then without it, and I cannot serve as a pastor and teacher—disciple of our Lord—NOW, without that time with God each day. He is our strength!

If we are going to lead our people and meet their needs—and equip them for ministry—we must again become a people of prayer and devotion ourselves. Surely this is the forgotten discipline and vital resource of faith to which we must return so that we might all be equipped for the ministry of love and service to which God calls us. It is imperative that we do this, for our very lives as Christians in a world of despair and doubt, depend on it. "The modern world has—an urgent need for a life of prayer. Unless the members of a technological society are also men of adoration and praise, technology will enslave and ultimately destroy them."[2] If we are to live as vital, caring, and serving disciples of Jesus Christ in and to our world, we have no recourse other than to come before our Father in prayer—in and through Jesus Christ our Lord. The very breath of life for a Christian is prayer. The old hymn says it well:

Prayer is the soul's sincere desire,
Unuttered or expressed,
The motion of a hidden fire
That trembles in the breast. . . .

Prayer is the Christian's vital breath,
The Christian's native air, . . .

O Thou, by whom we come to God,
The Life, the Truth, the Way;
The path of prayer thyself hast trod:
Lord, teach us how to pray!

—James Montgomery

Jesus Christ, as Son of God, was a man of prayer and spent long hours, often all night, in prayer to His Father. He instructs us to pray as He did. We are to follow in His steps—if we are to receive His Spirit to empower us as servant-disciples.

Though I have come to believe in prayer, it has been difficult for me to understand and practice a life of prayer. All of us are so much a part of modern secular humanity that we have the innate desire to control and direct our own lives. Even the thought of being completely dependent on—or waiting before God—for Him to speak to us and guide us goes against the very grain of our desire for independence and freedom. For a long time I was troubled and found it difficult to understand how my praying to God could or should, make a difference in His action.

Several years ago I voiced my doubts and honestly stated my reservations concerning the efficacy of prayer, especially with regard to divine healing, to one of the great missionary statesmen of our time. Dr. Frank Laubach said to me, "Ira, you don't understand prayer. You do not turn God on in prayer. You open your life to God in trust and obedience and make yourself available to Him. God is only waiting to use you as a channel for His love and power when you make yourself available!" Make oneself available! Wait on God! He is waiting on you!

Yet those who wait for the Lord
Will gain new strength;
They will mount up with wings like eagles,
They will run and not get tired,
They will walk and not become weary.

(Isa. 40:31)

Coming to God with all my needs and weaknesses—with all my sins and failures—waiting on Him—prayer! Then and then only, God meets my need, forgives my sins and failures, and gives me His strength for my weakness. It is only by the presence, the power, and the strength of God Himself that we will be liberated for witness and ministry. When we make ourselves available to God, He uses us as His channels and instruments to do great and wonderful things. Prayer now makes sense to me; it is the way for me to receive God's forgiveness, grace, power, and love. It is in and through His Spirit in prayer, as a child to His Father, a fellow-heir with Jesus Christ, that I am then equipped to love and serve others and to help equip them for ministry.

The ministry of which I talk is not just going to church—being saved for eternal life—and living a good moral life. No, it is much more than that. It is giving one's life and risking to touch the wounds of others, as one who knows what it is to be wounded and healed by God's Spirit and love. It is going into the world where people are hurting and hungry, hungry in body and heart, and not only providing a cup of cold water and a piece of bread in His name, but also introducing them to the presence of the One who lives today as Savior and Lord. It is witness and ministry, dependent on the grace of God and empowered by the gift of God's Spirit and equipped by the gifts of the Spirit. And, it does work where it is tried in a local church. In the next chapter we shall talk about that!

X

The Church in Witness and Ministry

And He put all things in subjection under His feet, and gave Him as head over all things to the church, which is His body, the fulness of Him who fills all in all. (Eph. 1:22-23)

Now you are Christ's body, and individually members of it. (I Cor. 12:27)

"Go therefore and make disciples of all the nations, baptizing them in the name of the Father and the Son and the Holy Spirit, teaching them to observe all that I commanded you; and lo, I am with you always, even to the end of the age."
(Matt. 28:19-20)

Any renewal of the church that occurs must happen in the local church—else it will be neither authentic nor lasting. The preachments and exhortation of few or many, on the national or general church level, have little effect or lasting value, unless the people of God in the local congregation live out the life of Christ as His body, the church, in witness and ministry.

It is also my conviction that the greatest weakness of the church does not come from radical social activists, radical evangelicals, or emotional charismatics. No, the greatest weakness of the church centers in on the vast majority of its members, including bishops, pastors, and other leaders of the church, who are neither evangelical nor activist enough and who are not truly open to the gift of the Holy Spirit or the gifts of the Spirit which are essential for witness and ministry. The nominal or cultural Christian, whether ordained or lay, who will not take seriously the radical claims of the gospel concerning salvation from sin, a life of discipleship, and stewardship of all of life in witness and ministry for Christ, represents the greatest weakness in the church today. This crippling weakness, along with the aberrations of those who stress a one-sided gospel of either "social action" or "pietism," can be overcome through the patient and persistent teaching and preaching of the whole gospel. Jesus Christ came teaching, preaching, and healing and He calls us to follow after Him. He says to us today, "As the Father has sent Me, I also send you" (John 20:21*b*).

In a number of local congregations within The United Methodist Church today people are responding to a holistic gospel and are living out the faith in a vital and life-changing manner. These are vibrant and growing people who consciously see themselves as Christ's church—the visible body of Christ—alive in the world today.

It is my privilege to serve one of these congregations which is becoming increasingly aware of and committed to the claims of the whole gospel. Many people in our local fellowship are beginning to see the world as our parish—and more importantly, a world that includes our own backyard. I could, without undue pride, point to what God is doing in the life and ministry of my own people in response to the radical claims of the biblical faith. Our congregation is one where renewal and Christian growth are taking place and where witness and mission are becoming more central in the faith commitments of many people. I have chosen, however, to use three congregations other than my own as examples of renewal of the "body-life" in the local congregation. These congregations include one downtown church, First United Methodist in Tulsa, Oklahoma; one large primarily ethnic congregation, Ben Hill United Methodist in Atlanta, Georgia; and one suburban church, First United Methodist in Carrollton, Texas.

In each of these congregations, Christ is preached as the head of the body, and the membership of the church is taught that they are members of that body. In addition, the doctrine of the Holy Spirit is taught as the real presence and power of God with us today, empowering all His people for witness and ministry. God is preached and experienced both as historically revealed in Jesus Christ and made powerfully present in the lives of Christ's disciples through the Holy Spirit. In addition, the life of worship and ministry of each of these congregations is marked by an air or sense of expectant faith in a redeeming God who will bring salvation, or wholeness, to life in the here and now, as well as the hereafter.

First, let us consider what has happened and is happening under the ministry and leadership of Dr. L. D. Thomas, Jr., at First United Methodist Church in Tulsa, Oklahoma. Fifteen years ago, in 1966, when Dr. Thomas was appointed to First Church, the membership of approximately 3,000 with an average Sunday worship attendance of 350 to 400 was declining. First Church was literally standing under the shadow of Boston Avenue United Methodist Church, just two blocks away, which at that time was the fifth largest church in Methodism. The sanctuary of the beautiful Tudor-Gothic cathedral building of First Church seats approximately 1,500. In 1966 the budget of the church was $134,000 and half of that was required to maintain the building and keep the doors open.

Dr. Thomas says, "When I was appointed to First Methodist, Tulsa, my friends and colleagues did not congratulate me; they consoled me. The first Finance

Committee meeting I attended, one week after my appointment, was for the purpose of seeing how we could cut $10,000 out of our budget; for there was no way we could raise the $134,000 we had budgeted." The membership of the church was continuing to grow in age and there were few young families. Dr. Thomas was the only full-time ordained minister on the staff.

Now, fifteen years later, let us see what has and is happening to an old downtown first church. By and large, all the sociological studies of church life in the last twenty years have depicted for "old first church" a very questionable future as a viable congregation. But, First Church, Tulsa, is not going the way of "old first church." Today, it has over 5,500 members with an average attendance in 1980 of over 2,300. Also in 1980 First Church led all churches in our denomination with 1,612 average attendance in church school.

Many young families regularly join First Church and now far outnumber the senior citizens. The operating budget of the church stands at $1,500,000, a block-and-a-half of property has been purchased for necessary parking, the entire church has been completely refurbished, and a new $5,000,000 educational and program building is under construction, with payment scheduled to be completed in three years. This building will include new kitchen facilities, a new meeting hall seating 800 people around tables for the pastor's weekly Bible study on Wednesday evening, and new classrooms for over 700 children under twelve years of age. Incidentally, the study of the Word of God, led by the teaching ministry of Pastor Thomas, is one of the primary ingredients of the significant renewal which has occurred at First Church. That teaching has been centered not only in the Bible as the Word of God, but also in the Holy Spirit as the living presence of God among us.

If you ask Dr. Thomas what has happened in the past fifteen years to generate such a change in First United Methodist Church, Tulsa, he will answer:

Why, that's simple! Our people have simply opened up their lives and permitted the Holy Spirit to minister to them! That's it. Period. Only the Holy Spirit can truly minister to people, and all we do as the clergy is to help create an atmosphere of faith where this can happen. We try to create this atmosphere in many ways, but everything we do adds up to three things:

1. We lift up Jesus Christ as God Himself in the flesh! Not as just a good man, or a good teacher, or the perfect example. But we proclaim Him as God who died on a cross to redeem us and who was raised from the dead and lives to be our Lord of life.
2. We preach and teach the Bible as the Word of God, not as just *containing* the Word of God, which you can figure out if you are smart enough and have enough education. But the Bible is God's Word for every person, regardless of education, when that person is willing to accept it as his own Word for living. Like John Wesley said, "We are truly a church of one book!"
3. The third way we create this atmosphere of faith is by helping our people actually experience the reality and the power of the Holy Spirit in their lives right now!

The growing witness and outreach ministry of First Church is so varied and extensive that I can sketch it only briefly here. I would encourage any person, whether minister or a layperson, who is interested in finding the secret of renewal for an old downtown church to carefully explore what is happening at First Church, Tulsa. Among its many ministries is a Christian Counseling Center staffed by an ordained minister, with a Ph.D. in counseling from Stanford, who came to the staff from the Tulsa Psychiatric Center. All the counselors are professionally trained. But there is one difference at this Christian Counseling Center; here, the Scriptures are used as the truth content for counseling. In addition, Dr. Thomas has a unique counseling program for the laity which is called, "The Ministry of Counseling Prayer." Some 120 laity are being trained to participate in the ministry of the Holy Spirit, bringing healing and wholeness through the body of Christ.

First Methodist of Tulsa has an extended healing ministry in which several hundred of its members work. These members are thoroughly trained in how to visit and pray for the sick. Laypeople in the church go to all five hospitals in Tulsa four days each week, visiting not only the members of First Methodist but also all Methodists from out of town. Other teams of laypeople visit in eighteen nursing homes in Tulsa each week, and still other teams visit regularly over three hundred shut-ins who belong to the church. On the third Sunday evening of each month a healing service is held in the sanctuary with Dr. Thomas officiating. He is assisted by three physicians: an orthopedic surgeon, a psychiatrist, and a general practitioner. The physicians help the congregation learn about the nature of a patient's illness and what is needed for a cure. This helps the congregation know how to pray for the sick. Many miraculous healings have occurred and been verified.

In the area of missions, First Church is growing and reaching out. It has formed a working partnership with the Methodist Church in Kenya. Dr. Thomas recently returned from a visit to Kenya, and his people responded to the many needs that he shared with them. First Church is now in the process of providing a gas system, a water system, a new maternity ward, and fourteen homes for medical personnel at the Maua Hospital in Meru, which is the center of Methodist work in Kenya. In addition they have committed themselves to build a training center for ministers, something that is badly needed in a conference of over five hundred Methodist churches with less than forty ordained clergy. Also, each year the members of First Church are underwriting the college education of four students from Kenya. It is the hope of Dr. Thomas and the people of First Church that their church can serve as a model for other churches (or districts), and form a partnership with a struggling national church in Africa, Asia, Central or South America. There is a truth here that is essential for future growth and support of world missions—people want to have direct relationships with those whom they join as partners in Christ's mission.

Locally, First Church finances a ministry of caring love to low-income apartment children. Many of these children are brought to the church one afternoon each week for tutoring by lay volunteers. Also, First Church pays the salary of an ethnic pastor who meets with the children each day after school.

Finally, concerning mission support in a time when there is such a great emphasis in the church on paying all apportionments, First Church pays the largest amount of apportionments and benevolences in the Oklahoma Conference. In addition, for the past ten years Dr. Thomas pledged to each of his district superintendents, "If any Methodist church in the Tulsa District cannot pay out [there are forty-five churches in the district] we at First Church will pay them out." This pledge has been faithfully kept. Surely the bishops and hierarchy of the church should want to encourage more of what is happening at First Church, Tulsa.

Incidentally, First Church can well be called evangelical, activist, and charismatic—certainly not a normal United Methodist church. Dr. Thomas considers one of the greatest and most meaningful accomplishments at First Church to be the way so-called charismatic Christians and traditional Christans accept one another, worship, and work together without dissension. Dr. Thomas says, "One of the greatest thrills I have each week comes following the pastoral prayer, when the congregation sings 'Alleluia,' and I look out over the congregation and see a charismatic standing there with his hands raised, side-by-side with a member who has been in our church fifty years and is worshiping in a traditional manner; and both loving each other and accepting each other as brothers and sisters in Christ."

In a time when polarization is occurring in many places about the ministry of the Holy Spirit in the church today, the pastors and ministers of First United Methodist in Tulsa are building bridges—bringing together a very diverse people as one people who name Jesus Christ as Lord. In their case, they would quickly say, "The Holy Spirit is the one who has brought us together and is the foundation and source of our unity."

Another congregation that is an example of an alive and vibrant people of God growing in faith and in membership is the great Ben Hill United Methodist Church in Atlanta, Georgia. Dr. Cornelius L. Henderson, the dynamic pastor there, combines in his ministry an emphasis on vital worship and biblical preaching along with a deep pastoral concern for his people. The one description that would be adequate enough to describe church life there is: Ben Hill is a place where people find the Word of God preached in a contemporary manner and experience an excitement and expectancy in worship that is seldom experienced elsewhere. It is truly a joy and an uplifting experience to worship at Ben Hill United Methodist Church.

Pastor Henderson came to Ben Hill Church in 1975 after serving several years as a staff member of the General Board of Discipleship. From his travels and preaching all over the continent and the world, Dr. Henderson knows the church and the needs of people. When he became its pastor Ben Hill was a church in transition. Formerly an "all white" congregation, the church is now almost an "all black" congregation. The membership in 1975 was under 300; now in mid-1981, it is over 2,300 and is growing weekly as people come to join on profession of faith and baptism, transfer from other United Methodist churches and from many other denominations. The church school is growing as is worship attendance.

There are two morning worship services at Ben Hill. The early service is a more traditional, structured period for those who find such an experience most meaningful for them. The later service is freer, less structured, and overflows into fellowship hall where those who arrive late can be a part of the service by means of closed circuit television. In 1975, church attendance stood at approximately 175 and church school attendance at approximately 80. On an average Sunday today, some 1,100 people worship and over 300 attend church school. Because of the overflow worship attendance, the congregation is now involved in a remodeling program to enlarge their sanctuary and to add other needed space. During the last six years the budget of Ben Hill has increased from under $60,000 to nearly $300,000 per year. In all aspects of its life, the Ben Hill congregation reflects growth and vitality.

The program and people of Ben Hill are certainly pluralistic. Both the social activist and the pietist can be found there, often in the same person, along with the evangelical and the charismatic. There is a sense of affirmation and acceptance among the people of Ben Hill. The motto of Ben Hill is, "Where everybody is somebody." The goal of the church stated in their new member booklet is:

To all who mourn and need comfort—
To all who are tired and need rest—
To all who are friendless and want friendship—
To all who are lonely and want companionship—
To all who are homeless and want sheltering love—
To all who sin and need forgiveness—
This Church opens wide its doors, and in the
name of Jesus Christ the Lord
says, *"Welcome."*

At Ben Hill, a concerted and intentional effort is made to acquaint new members with The United Methodist Church, its polity, history, and doctrine, and with the life of Ben Hill in particular. The new member booklet gives specific details about the various programs of study and ministry. It is expected that the congregation and its staff will help or enable each person to find his or her place in the life of the church as a means of fulfilling the motto and goals of the church. Dr. Henderson says, "This church is a Christ-centered, people-oriented church, where truly everybody is somebody, and Christ is lifted up as the head."

In its new member orientation, the people at Ben Hill are sensitive to those who have selected them as their new church family. The first session of the class for new members deals with the desires and expectations of the incoming members—what are their needs and what do they look for in ministry of the church to them. The second session deals with the church's expectation of its membership. Ben Hill is indeed fortunate to have Dr. Major Jones, the head of Gammon Theological Seminary, as one of its leaders. He lectures on the nature of the church, bringing a sound theological base for discipleship in the church. The third session deals with the polity and structure of the Methodist tradition and emphasizes the advantage and positive benefits of being a connectional church—a church that is both catholic and reformed in its roots. The fourth session looks at the ministry and life of Ben Hill and shows the dreams and visions of the church.

Behind and undergirding all of this is a committed and innovative pastor. As Dr. Major Jones states it, "For a church to be as alive as Ben Hill is, a dynamic and caring pastor-preacher is a must." Dr. Henderson is practicing in his own life what is absolutely essential if the ethnic minority local church is to grow. He is giving dedicated leadership to the local church. He has left the institutional position with the title and perks that go with such a position and is giving his life and ministry to bringing renewal to the church—in the only place were it can truly be renewed, at the local level.

Ben Hill is a family-oriented church, but it does not place all the emphasis on the nuclear family. With many single-parent families, a growing social fact in our time, much stress is placed on the church as family. In other words, anyone can belong at Ben Hill and find a place there. I do not ever recall a greater sense of belonging and affirmation than my wife and I personally received in a regular communion worship service at Ben Hill. We truly felt a part of the body of Christ in the central sacramental act of worship, Holy Communion.

Sometimes it might appear that Ben Hill is all music—or all choir. It has a sanctuary choir, a gospel choir, an agape choir, a bell choir, a male chorus, a C. L. Henderson quartet, an instrumental ensemble, a youth choir, a children's choir, and a cherub choir. It seems that everyone at Ben Hill *sings* the gospel! The result is great participation in worship, exciting and uplifting music—both instrumental and vocal—and the sharing of God's Spirit and love through a wide variety of good and meaningful music.

People come to Ben Hill because they are accepted and affirmed in God's family. Further, something is happening there—Jesus Christ is preached as Lord and the reality of God is experienced as empowering Holy Spirit. Surely, such a people make a difference as they live out their lives in the secular world around them. Ben Hill United Methodist Church is a symbol of hope and expectation for the renewal of the local church in our day.

We have looked at dynamic renewal in an old downtown First Church where a dying church has come alive and is growing in witness and ministry in a remarkable way. We have looked at a church that has moved through a transition period in membership and is now one of the vibrant and alive primarily ethnic churches in America. Next, let us take a look at the suburban scene, the renewal and growth as experienced in the First United Methodist Church in Carrollton, Texas, an affluent and growing suburb of Dallas.

As the history of churches go in Texas, First Church Carrollton has a long history. It was founded as a part of a circuit, following a brush arbor meeting in 1901. In 1967, the Reverend Kenneth Carter, a graduate of Perkins School of Theology, was appointed to Carrollton as his second pastorate. A former army captain and young Ford executive,

Ken had left a secular vocation and entered the ministry in 1962. As he leads the ministry at Carrollton, Ken comments, "I think affluence always retards the spread of the gospel. People are caught up in leading the 'good life' so much that they are not seeking out God or the church, and miss the *truly* Good Life. They have to be shown through God's love their need for God." First Church Carrollton has one of the most effective and intentional evangelistic commitments of any church in America to seek out people and share with them God's love in Jesus Christ.

The staff and lay leadership of the church have meshed an active evangelistic program with a wide variety of relational ministries to provide nurture and growth to a rapidly growing congregation. The church provides many ministries and opportunities, what they call a "cafeteria" approach, so that people who want to grow and mature in their faith can find something that will minister to them at the level of their own spiritual life.

In 1967, when Ken and Freddie Carter were assigned to Carrollton, the congregation was lethargic and divided. The church had a membership of some 900 people with an average attendance at worship of approximately 260 and a church school attendance of some 290. It had a total budget for all purposes of some $54,000. It paid its apportionments but gave only minimal amounts to other askings or advance special gifts of the church. Today, this alive and growing congregation has 2,600 members, regularly has 1,200 to 1,300 in worship, and over 1,100 on the average each Sunday in church school. It is one of a dozen or so United Methodist congregations in America with a church school of over 1,000 in attendance.

First Church has an annual budget of approximately $1,250,000 and meets in a new sanctuary seating some 1,000 people. Their Sunday morning church school is rapidly outgrowing its space and the church is growing in second-mile giving through mission specials. It has passed the $100,000 mark in giving beyond its apportioned benevolences. Incidentally, the conference apportionments and church-wide benevolences at First Church are all paid 100 percent in ten monthly installments through the year. Members of this church not only take care of their own, but they reach out to others with their caring love.

How did all of this happen? How did a church, even in a growing suburb, triple its membership, quadruple its attendance in church and church school, and become dynamically alive in ministry and mission, while at the same time United Methodism across the nation was losing over 1,000,000 members and showing a steady decline in attendance at worship and church school? Let us look at that picture.

The evangelistic tool at First Church Carrollton is based on a deep commitment to Jesus Christ as Savior and Lord—and on the Great Commission, as structured in Evangelism Explosion. Probably more than any other United Methodist church minister, Ken with his staff has used Evangelism Explosion and adopted it for the congregation in the Methodist tradition. In a ten-year period over 2,000 people were trained to share the gospel with others. Ken, as senior-pastor, stays involved in the teaching program of Evangelism Explosion, personally teaching at least one of three classes meeting weekly in two fourteen-week courses each year.

The results of this intentional evangelism program showed an average of 260 members per year joining First Church in the decade of the 70s, with a net gain in membership of over 100 per year. Particularly significant is the record of those received on profession of faith: 175 in 1979, and 186 in 1980—leading the North Texas Conference in both years. During this time morning worship grew by 750 members and church school attendance by 622. Remember, this is a time when membership and attendance in worship and Sunday school were on a steady decline in The United Methodist Church.

In addition to exciting worship services and a growing

church school, there is much teaching and nurturing of the congregation during the week, especially on Wednesday evenings, when hundreds of families come to the church to be taught. After a family meal is shared, classes are offered for the entire family, covering Bible teaching, family living, finances, and special classes on Methodism, the Holy Spirit, and Bible studies, taught by the senior pastor. The minister of education believes in teaching teachers to teach and employs the Bethel Bible Series for this purpose. Both he and the pastor's wife, Freddie, personally teach small leadership classes of 25 or less. These intensively trained teachers (a four-year commitment required), then become the teachers of the Bethel Bible Series on the congregational level. Other aspects of education include midweek clubs for girls (Pioneer Girls) and boys (Boys Brigade). Women meet for home Bible studies during the day, and couples meet in the evenings. Retreats, revivals, and seminars led by guest speakers give fresh views in the teaching areas. Vacation Bible school and day camp for older elementary boys and girls provide a setting during the summer where the gospel can be shared by specially trained teachers, with the emphasis being on ministry to the community by inviting all to come. Special classes for the deaf and handicapped are available. A new family with a son suffering from cerebral palsy commented that they joined First Church primarily because of the acceptance they and their son felt in just a couple of worship services. Wheelchairs are a very familiar sight in the corridors of the church. Special architectural consideration in the new buildings and planned expansions provide easy access for the handicapped to enter, leave, and use restrooms.

Strong biblical preaching with a continuing and ongoing teaching and discipling midweek program builds a church with a vital witness and ministry. In addition to the more than $100,000 in second-mile support, the church expends over $15,000 annually in emergency funds to aid members and nonmembers who come to the church in a time of crisis or special need. The Reverend Carter is quick to point out that the real foundation for the strong stewardship record at First Church is a positive emphasis on proportional giving. Members, as growing disciples, are urged to step up in their giving each year until they are tithing—not as a legal requirement but as evidence of their gratitude for God's wonderful mercy and love.

The following story illustrates the caring ministry of the church in a graphic way. Through the loving outreach of a Sunday school class, a shy young couple with two small children was gradually involved in the total ministry care of the church. Through an Evangelism Explosion presentation in the home, both wife and husband made commitments to the Lord. After approximately one year in a Sunday school class, through patient love, the extremely quiet and shy husband was won over to the point that he felt comfortable in sharing himself and in relating to others in the church. The wife had preceded him in these feelings and was an active volunteer in the church office. After a hospital stay, and much testing, it was discovered that the young man had leukemia. During the remaining two years of his life, he became president of the Sunday school class, ushered on Sunday mornings, and shared his witness both on the job and in the neighborhood. During the long months of therapy, the Sunday school class supported the family by caring for the children, providing meals, visiting the hospital, praying, and teaching the young couple, so new in the faith. Shortly before his death, the man made a public witness to his class of his love for his wife and deep appreciation of her love for him, and for the love of his "classmates" and the church. After his death, the class again pitched in to repair, repaint, plumb, and secure the house for his young widow. Car repairs were also made. The church emergency fund made payments to the hospital for the 20 percent of the bill that was not covered by insurance. The wife always maintained a thankful spirit for all that the Lord, friends, neighbors, and church members had done for her, so when insurance settlements came, the wife insisted, over protests of some members of her family, that a tenth of the money go to her church. The wife continues to minister in her church as a valued volunteer.

Many more such stories could be told and such love is catching and growing at First United Methodist Church in Carrollton, Texas. This spirit of commitment and generosity ensuing in servant ministry is contagious and has given rise to the slogan or motto of the 1981 stewardship campaign, "People-Touching Ministries." And, people want to be where their needs are being met—where others genuinely care about them. The following quote from a recent stewardship brochure, "People Touching Ministries," sums up the spirit of the people of First Church.

Loving and caring is what we are all about at First United Methodist Church Carrollton. Jesus entrusted to the Christians the care of the lost and hurting world. We seek always to carry our share of this task.

Because Jesus loves us and gives us strength, we can love others and touch them in a real way which gives them strength. At First Church, we worship together, study and pray together, talk over problems, share dreams, frustrations, successes and failures. We grow together, learning to be a witness for Jesus in the world, and then we go out and touch others who hurt.

Maybe you don't know the loving touch of Jesus Christ. . . . we want to help you find it! If you do know the loving touch of Jesus Christ, we want to help you share it!

How can we help you? and how can you help us? . . . touch the world for Jesus. . . .

As I reflect on what I have written in this book about the urgent need to liberate the church for witness and ministry, I am renewed in my own conviction that the local church is the key place where renewal and new life must occur. From my own experience, I know that God can and will renew the life of a congregation if a basic biblical pattern is followed. There must be strong biblical preaching in which the forgiving and reconciling mercy of a loving God is held forth as the sure answer to humanity's sin, greed, and estrangement. The people of God need again to learn, through disciplined study, the unique story of God's relationship with a called and covenant people as recorded in the Old and New Testaments. Christians desperately need to understand themselves today as a people called to be in covenant with God, both redeemed by God and sent forth by Him in witness and ministry to the world. This requires long and patient teaching by the pastor and lay leadership. Finally, the church needs again to see itself as dramatically the body of Christ, empowered by the Holy Spirit, with the gifts of the Holy Spirit for witness and ministry. Surely, in United Methodism and much of the rest of the church, the Holy Spirit has been the forgotten third person of the Trinity for too many years. But through trusting faith in Jesus Christ, and openness to the Holy Spirit, the church can again be renewed and liberated for witness and ministry to the world.

The three churches which I have used as examples all evidence strong biblical preaching, a caring and teaching ministry, and a trusting openness to the Holy Spirit. Each one, in a somewhat different way, offers vivid and striking evidence that any local church can come alive—grow—and serve others in God's world.

God's saving love is still available to all who will open their lives to Him. God's empowering Spirit is present to equip us for witness and ministry. It is only in response to that love and obedience to His Spirit that we can expect to be renewed—and liberated for witness and ministry. Please, Lord, let it be so! Amen and amen!

Notes

Introduction

1. Samuel M. Shoemaker, *With the Holy Spirit and with Fire* (New York: Harper & Brothers, 1960), p. 40.
2. Albert C. Outler, ed., *John Wesley* (New York: Oxford University Press, 1964), p. 72.

Chapter I

1. Richard M. Weaver, *Ideas Have Consequences* (Chicago: University of Chicago Press, 1948), p. 4.
2. C. S. Lewis, *The Case for Christianity* (New York: The Macmillan Co., 1956), p. 45.
3. Thomas C. Oden, *Agenda for Theology* (New York: Harper & Row, 1979), p. 118.

Chapter II

1. C. Peter Wagner, *What We Are Missing?* (Carol Stream, Ill.: Creation House, 1973), pp. 16-18.
2. Howard A. Snyder, *The Problem of Wineskins* (Downers Grove, Ill.: Inter-Varsity Press, 1975), p. 158.

Chapter III

1. Paul C. Vitz, *Psychology as Religion: The Cult of Self-Worship* (Grand Rapids: Eerdmans Publishing Co., 1977).

2. *Ibid.*, p. 11.
3. *Ibid.*, p. 12.
4. *Ibid.*, p. 9.
5. *Ibid.*, p. 91.
6. Russell Kirk, *Enemies of the Permanent Things* (Westport, Ct.: Arlington House, 1969), Sinnot quote, pp. 161-62.
7. Richard F. Lovelace, *Dynamics of Spiritual Life: An Evangelical Theology of Renewal* (Downers Grove, Ill.: Inter-Varsity Press, 1979), p. 285.

Chapter IV

1. John Wesley, *The Character of a Methodist, From the 'Works' of John Wesley* (London: The Epworth Press, 1950 edition), pp. 7, 15.
2. *The Book of Worship for Church and Home* (Nashville: The United Methodist Publishing House, 1964), p. 12.
3. *The United Methodist Newscope*, The National Weekly Newsletter for United Methodist Leaders, 8 (November 21, 1980), 2.
4. Outler, *John Wesley*, p. 92.
5. *The Book of Discipline of The United Methodist Church* (Nashville: The United Methodist Publishing House, 1980), p. 78.
6. Wesley, *The Character of a Methodist*, pp. 7, 9.
7. Outler, *John Wesley*, pp. 101-2.

Chapter V

1. Wesley, *The Character of a Methodist*, p. 8.
2. *The Book of Discipline*, p. 203.
3. Vitz, *Psychology as Religion*, p. 36.
4. *Ibid.*, pp. 88-89.

Chapter VI

1. Orlando Patterson, "Hidden Dangers in the Ethnic Revival," *New York Times*, February 20, 1978.
2. John Wesley, *The Standard Sermons*, 3rd ed., ed. Edward H. Sugden (London: The Epworth Press, 1951), Sermon XLIV, p. 310.
3. *Ibid.*, pp. 314-27.
4. *Ibid.*, p. 311.

Chapter VII

1. "The Church in Our Day," a pastoral letter, American Roman Catholic Bishops, January 1968, chapter 1.
2. Sharon Mielke, "UMC Lacks Will to Change, Poll Says," *The United Methodist Reporter*, January 25, 1980, p. 3.
3. Sharon Mielke, "Scholar Says Founder Would 'Disown' UMC," *The United Methodist Reporter*, August 1, 1980, p. 4.

4. *The United Methodist Newscope,* 5 (March 25, 1977), 1.
5. Clyde Chestnut, *The United Methodist Reporter,* April 27, 1979, p. 3.
6. Albert C. Outler, "Facing UMC'S Accountability Crisis," *The Circuit Rider,* 3 (November/December 1979), 8.
7. *The Book of Discipline,* p. 35.
8. Outler, "Facing UMC'S Accountability Crisis," pp. 8-9.
9. *Ibid.,* p. 9.
10. Richard M. Weaver, *Visions of Order* (Baton Rouge, La.: Louisiana State University Press, 1964), pp. 53-54.
11. Howard Snyder, *The Radical Wesley* (Downers Grove, Ill.: Inter-Varsity Press, 1980), p. 72.

Chapter VIII

1. Peter L. Berger, "The Class Struggle in American Religion," *The Christian Century* (February 25, 1981), 194, 196.
2. David Jessup, *Preliminary Inquiry Regarding Financial Contributions to Outside Political Groups by Boards and Agencies of The United Methodist Church, 1977-79* (April 7, 1980).
3. *Ibid.,* p. 1.
4. *The Use of Money in Mission—an Opportunity for Understanding,* United Methodist Communications brochure (October 17, 1980), 3.
5. David Jessup, *Reply to United Methodist Brochure* (November 10, 1980).
6. James and Margaret Goff, *In Every Person Who Hopes* (New York: Friendship Press, 1980), pp. 55-56.
7. Rusty Davenport, "Cuba: A Land of Contrasts," *Common Ground,* a Newsletter of the United Methodist Voluntary Service, 3/4 (Summer 1981), 14.
8. *Ibid.*
9. *Ibid.,* pp. 15-16.
10. Alexander Solzhenitsyn and others, *From Under the Rubble* (Boston: Little, Brown, 1975), pp. 14, 24-25.
11. *Ibid.,* p. 81.
12. *Ibid.,* pp. 145-47.

Chapter IX

1. *The Book of Discipline,* p. 212.
2. Michel Quoist, *The Meaning of Success* (Notre Dame, Ind.: Fides Publishers, 1965), p. 219.